One of Britain's most celebrated comedy writers and producers, Armando Iannucci is a creator of *Veep, The Day Today, Alan Partridge, The Friday Night Armistice, Time Trumpet* and *The Thick of It*. He has produced many TV and radio programmes, and is the director of the movies *In the Loop* and *The Death of Stalin*. His previous book, *The Audacity of Hype*, was also published by Little, Brown.

Hear me Out

All my Music

ARMANDO IANNUCCI

Little, Brown

LITTLE, BROWN

This collection first published in Great Britain in 2017 by Little, Brown

1 3 5 7 9 10 8 6 4 2

A CIP catalogue record for this book is
available from the British Library.

ISBN 978-1-4087-0988-7

Typeset in Palatino by M Rules
Printed and bound in Great Britain by
Clays Ltd, St Ives plc

Papers used by Little, Brown are from well-managed forests
and other responsible sources.

Little, Brown
An imprint of
Little, Brown Book Group
Carmelite House
50 Victoria Embankment
London EC4Y 0DZ

An Hachette UK Company
www.hachette.co.uk

www.littlebrown.co.uk

*I'd like to dedicate this to three people
who very kindly heard me out: James Inverne, who
commissioned me to write for* **Gramophone** *magazine;
Jessica Isaacs, who encouraged me to talk about music
on Radio 3; and David Sawer, who patiently and
generously added my words to his music.*

Contents

Introduction

Music seems to me the most tangible of imaginative acts and yet it isn't really there. Sure, you can touch a sculpture, carry a book and hang a painting, but no matter how magnificently these physical artefacts stimulate the senses or imagination, none of them can bring a dead person back to life. For me, music does exactly that. I'm not crazy. I don't believe in ghosts, and I'm not arguing there's a pseudo-mystical dimension in music. It's just that music often feels to me like the expression of someone's living thought.

Maybe because it's wordless it seems somehow a more convincing realisation of how an individual thinks and feels. The truth is, we never really think in coherent sentences. Instead, our brains seem to know what we mean the instant we begin the formation of an idea. We can see arguments in front of us before we voice them, and we start speaking sentences and working out what we mean as we go along.

Thoughts, then, really aren't verbal, not at their earliest stages anyway, when they spark. They're a vague, shapeless and intangible mass of ideas that still quite convincingly claim to make sense. And that's how I regard music. It's just noise, choreographed sounds – notes, clatter, harmony, bangs and beats – that strangely seem to mean something, say something even. It feels like a language. Noises shoved around in a pattern or rhythm, which then spark and start evoking sadness, excitement, apprehension or one of another hundred urges in the mind of the listener. More than that, many millions of us agree on what those urges are. We all know when a piece of music sounds melancholy, or when it's uplifting, yet the music itself is totally abstract. Why is that?

Why is it that just by making notes go higher, or quieter or faster, a meaning forms inside us to give shape or sense to what we're hearing?

Whatever the explanation – if there is one at all – music makes me feel I'm in the company of something living. It feels to me like hearing someone's voice; their personality seems in the room.

Why classical music, though? Maybe it's just my contrary nature. I used to share a bedroom with a brother who was into Lou Reed and Deep Purple. I always remember thinking, I don't get this. Then, aged thirteen, at a musical appreciation class at school, when the teacher played an old vinyl recording of Holst's *The Planets*, I instantly froze. I got it. That's the sound I wanted to hear but couldn't describe because until then I'd never heard it before. That noise – a full symphony orchestra – dramatic, emotional, yet so much more than those labels suggest. The fact that there were no words, no visuals, made it seem more suggestive and real. There was something potent about its abstraction. *The Planets* does of course have a sort of programme, in that the seven sections are seven musical portraits of the classical gods the planets are named after. But, other than the lead emotion, nothing more is described. And that's what I find so enticing. That pure noise can seem to make a story or utter a narrative.

When I was about fourteen a new library opened down the road from us in Glasgow, with an amazingly comprehensive classical music record section. Soon I found myself pursuing those big abstract sounds, massive symphonies from Mahler and Shostakovich, bizarre noises from modern composer like Ligeti and Xenakis, or ostensibly meaningless but amazingly meaningful patterns of sounds from Bach.

At that stage, I wasn't really into words with music. My father came from Naples, and opera was always on very loudly every weekend, usually Verdi or Puccini. I never got into it. It still seemed to me not as rich as the peculiarly indefinable language that purely instrumental music could utter. These were therefore my first tentative steps at becoming a pretentious twat.

I hope I've changed. I like Verdi and Puccini now, especially live. And I can see why Lou Reed is so admired. And my classical musical tastes have grown richer listening to vocal music, such as the magnificent choral works of Thomas Tallis or the song cycles of Schumann and Benjamin Britten, and to the far more intimate soundscape of chamber pieces, such as the amazing and mysterious string quartets by Béla Bartók. That's been the joy of my musical journey: it's a constantly expanding exploration, each discovery suggesting a fresh direction of travel, one new piece taking me to another, another composer, another genre, another time. Sometimes it's shocking to think I'll never finish. Other times, that's what's most thrilling about it; that this so-called 'dead' music is so amazingly alive.

Over the years, I find myself wanting to write about music.

Nothing on theory or analysis, but about what it does to the listener. In the process, I've also wanted to chip away at the veneer of pretention or irksome exclusivity that mounts such a forbidding entrance to classical music for anyone who wants to explore it for the first time. Much of the writing in this book is prompted by my belief this music is so special that anything which encourages or advises others to listen to it is always worth doing, and anything that tries to put them off should be spat at.

This isn't a manual, there's no structure, no Step 1, Step 2. Neither are there any specialist preparations required. My musical journey has been a mess, an erratic jump from one work to another. I'm glad it's been that way, and that's how I'd like to reflect it.

But this book is also an act of defiance. When so much of the world tells me to love something more 'contemporary', when it's shouting at me that I'm just not cool and I'll infect the company of anyone I'm in touching distance of with my clodhopping anachronistic and toxic lack of hip if I keep listening to the music of Henry Purcell, I just feel obliged to go and do it anyway. I keep meeting people like this all the time, people so battered by the collective imperative only to admit liking what the whole world is telling you to like, that they sneak out to classical lunchtime concerts with all the guilt of a Victorian clergyman desperately hunting a crack den. I've also been in polite small-talk going nowhere when suddenly a reference to classical music, to maybe a piece we both discover we know and like, gets us animated like two long-lost friends.

All my days, I've felt pressurised by the anonymous Keepers of the Cool who tell us what we should be wearing this year, what digital boxsets we should bunker ourselves in to enjoy, what amazing app is the only one we should be shrieking emotions at our recently acquired friends with. Thankfully, I have the one consolation that if I don't quite fit into all of this, everyone else probably feels the same way.

So, I say defiantly, I get more moved and excited by classical music than by any other musical genre. This is not to say that all classical music is equally glorious (try listening to more than two minutes of Stravinsky's *Les noces* without wanting to ram something with a hammer) but what I rejoice in is its depth. How can anything so complex be so utterly pure and beautiful? Go to any major orchestral concert and just look at the sheer welter of talent congregating on stage. Each one of the seventy or so musicians represents seventy or so hard-won careers of training and endless practice and amazing technical skill and dozens of heartbreaking moments along the way; each instrument is the product of centuries of design trial and error. The orchestra is such a magnificent folly: all that effort, to do what? To make noises in evening wear.

It's worth it for those noises, and I love it that they're complicated. I love it that you can never take in a piece of classical music on just one listening. Sure, you can be affected by it, be moved or intrigued by that first encounter. But what I love is the mental addiction: the need to hear it again, and again, before you can even begin to understand all its benefits. I love the fact that, thirty or so years on from first listening to Mahler's 9th Symphony, or Shostakovich's 10th, or Elgar's 1st, I'm still hearing wonderful moments in those pieces for the first time.

This is not to deride all other forms of music as lightweight in comparison. It's marvellous we have so much easy access to so many forms of music now (though sad that children are given fewer opportunities to explore them any further) but I'm badgering you now about classical music because I get rather frustrated that such a magnificent and rewarding invention is often ignored, derided even, as something not for the likes of us.

I knew someone who wouldn't let anyone go into her front living room, not even herself. It was kept 'For best'. We would end up having tea sitting in a row of folding plastic chairs in her narrow kitchen. That's what I feel we do with classical music: set it aside and block it off, keeping it for best. The black tie and evening dress paraphernalia that goes with it doesn't help. The large opera houses and stuccoed egos of some of those on the stage add to the exclusivity. Sadly, a great invention is roped off from the public. Classical music seems to us music you can listen to by invitation only.

It's also burdened with a technical language which can seem off-putting to a first-time listener. Programme notes referring to 'obbligato' and 'rallentando' can sometimes read like a detailed medical report doctors have issued to a patient just to make them feel stupid and incurably ill.

Whenever I write about music, the only commitment I ask of the reader is that they listen. Listening isn't always an easy option. Listening requires concentration and patience. But so does brushing your teeth or crossing the road. Classical music is often associated with difficulty: yet surely concentrating on one thing at a time should be one of the easiest things in the world. Why have your mind flooded with a mass of sensations, memories, information, worries, instructions and stimulation, when it can, for once, focus on one thing, a simple line of sound, maybe a short seven- or eight-minute movement of an orchestra, three minutes or so of a solo instrument or voice? And why not then get more ambitious, once used to the method of emptying your mind of all distractions, and concentrate solely and directly on a whole fifty-minute symphony?

Maybe because we have a limitless supply of artistic content thrown at us online now, we've forgotten how to make time and room for just one thing, and one thing alone. Maybe we've forgotten how to make listening an activity rather than a passive and indiscriminatory receiver of all the music pumped out at us from train station, shopping mall, cinema popcorn kiosk, musty cloakroom, taxiing airplane, TV junction point and sweaty exercise class. So, this is a polite, though loud, request from me to you that you don't feel frightened by the prospect of listening to this music.

I've been lucky enough to be asked to work closely with composers and musicians on various projects, sitting in on a soundtrack recording for a feature film I directed, writing programme notes for a concert, and spending quite some time crafting a carefully rhyming libretto for a comic opera. You'll read about some of these efforts in this book. I was also lucky to be invited to write a regular column for *Gramophone* magazine – some of which are gathered here – and I'd like to thank it's then editor James Irvine for giving me such a fabulous environment in which to sound off. Most recently, I was very fortunate to have been made patron of a small charity called Apollo Music Projects. These are professional musicians who go into inner-city schools in London, often to places where the budgets have been cut so much that there simply aren't the resources for basic music tuition or appreciation, and there they play. They sit as a string quartet in a classroom, and play and talk about complex music such as Haydn, Beethoven and Shostakovich. And the kids are mesmerised, because they are not being talked down to, because what they are hearing is complex in the way that most things we really like, dramas, games, novels, are complex.

At one point, the children are invited to touch the instruments while they're being played, to feel directly how the acoustics of, say, a cello work. This to me sums up what I believe about classical music: that it's there for us all, inviting us to reach out and touch it.

Use Your Ears

How do you listen to classical music? Are you a purist? Do you sit in absolute stillness, perhaps with the lights off, the rest of the family banished from the room and your headphones on to exclude extraneous noise?

Are you still bothered by the clock ticking? A shudder from the fridge? The dog barking to be let back in the house? Your neighbours, out in the street, talking about switching to faster broadband? Can you just make out the noise of a favourite cousin leaving a very, very long message on the answer machine? One that sounds quite urgent and possibly dreadful.

Today, we have the opportunity to listen to music more intently than ever before. There's now an almost unspoken instruction that, as we listen, we ought to do so perfectly and with unspoilt focus. But there's no recognition here that that's not really what happens.

It's more likely you'll have music on in the background as a pleasant soundtrack to other things. While you cook or eat dinner. Or get on with some work – maybe marking papers that will lead to the expulsion of a pupil. Or driving to Hull.

Or it'll be playing while you have an argument with British Telecom, or pick a dropped sausage off the floor, or unblock the bath. If there's an art to listening, it's one no one is ever going to perfect. Just as there's no one definitive performance of a piece, so there's no single ideal condition in which to hear it. Yet whilst most music critics are happy to talk about aspects of performance, very few would consider writing a review that noted how they listened, starting, for example: 'The Bavarian Symphony Orchestra were in splendid form for Prokofiev's Sixth, though I lost concentration in the second movement when I suddenly realised I'd forgotten our wedding anniversary.' Why not? How and when and where we listen all make as fundamental a contribution to a piece of music as, say, the instrumentation. Or style of playing. Or skill of the performer.

Listening has a relatively short history. Music was originally written to dance to, or as an act of devotion, or to march or mourn to. Or to play among family and friends. The idea of paying money just to listen is only a couple of hundred years old. Listening alone in the living room, or car, or jogging – even more recent.

Prince Esterházy, paying for a house orchestra and composer, in the form of Haydn, to come up with a regular output of symphonies, was the nearest the eighteenth century came to Spotify. And it was very exclusive.

I'm interested in the art of listening, because when it comes to music I have no other resources to call upon, being unable to sing, play, or tap in time. Yet I'm not alone in cherishing listening as the art form most likely to move me. The one which in fact causes the greatest physical changes in me, to my heart rate and body temperature. To how I move my limbs. To what I'm thinking. So I'm intrigued by what happens to us when we listen. Why is it different from what happens when we watch, or smell, or taste, or feel?

According to David Hargreaves, a developmental psychologist who specialises in music, there's something innate in music – a deep structure that triggers activity in the brains of anyone who hears it, whether they're from Cheshire or Chad.

He says, 'Psychologists like me have done studies where they've deliberately manipulated the tempo of music in shops, and measured things like the speed with which people walk around in them. Or even, in restaurants and in bars, the speed of eating and drinking. There's a study by my colleague Adrian North and me, done in a restaurant, and we find that the speed of the music can determine how quickly people eat and drink. And that the style of music can actually affect people's spending. If you play different kinds of music on different days in a restaurant, as we did over a two-week period, you find that people's spending patterns are different. They spend more money on the brandy, and more on the sweet and so on if you have certain types of music . . .'

It's now dawned on me why tickets to the opera cost so much. It's because, when you go to the ticket office, they pump out opera from the tannoy. Which makes you happy to spend eighty pounds for a tremendous view of a pillar.

At the risk of citing a controversial distinction, I think popular music affects us differently from classical music because we listen to these genres differently. Popular music is about spotting instant resonances; picking up on how it connects you to the period in which it was written, maybe even to your memories of when and where you first heard it. You can tell a piece of music was written in the 1960s or

1970s or mid-90s, and part of the pleasure derived from it is in hearing it celebrate its own sixties-ness, or whatever.

Classical music operates differently, I think. You don't listen to Wagner's opera *Parsifal* simply because you remember the first time you heard it, or because it's *so* mid-nineteenth-century German. Though these peculiarities are still there, the pleasure comes from something else. Something which, at the risk of sounding mystical, is more timeless. Placeless.

Very often we stay locked into the popular music of the decade in which we grew up. My generation will still be listening to Phil Collins twenty years from now. But with classical music, we feel less inhibited. More promiscuous in allowing ourselves to listen to sounds produced over a span of four hundred years or so.

But to talk of the fundamental mystery of music makes my enquiry sound a little more profound than it need be. In fact, any tendency to make music sound like some mystical, spiritual other-worldly essence can be instantly dispersed once you go and see music performed live. It's the most earthy, physical thing. Horn-players empty their instruments of spit. Violinists fret at snapping strings. Pianists moan and shiver and crouch and sniff loudly at the slow bits. Double-bassists look faintly ridiculous wrestling with a huge wooden coffin that's possibly about to engulf them. Music is actually a pull between the abstract and the physical, and listening is fraught with this tension too; a tension between the desire to listen attentively and the knowledge that conditions are always imperfect. But today, are these conditions exerting a more powerful pull?

I'm writing with Bach's *Well-Tempered Clavier* playing at home. I'm not listening to it, because I'm thinking: 'What on earth am I going to write?' But at this moment I'd prefer to have Bach than anything else, and played by Sviatoslav Richter because that's how I first heard and got to know the music.

But think how rude I'm being to Bach and Richter. Would we treat people the same way, who had other great talents to offer? If a ballet company came to perform in the work canteen, would we ignore them? We can park out on the street and leave the radio on while we pop into a shop to buy some sandwiches, but we'd never think of hiring a choir to perform outside a bakery. But that's how cursorily we treat music. It's as if we used the British Museum just as a place to dump our coats.

So, with so much music around, why aren't we really listening? It's been estimated that about 43 per cent of our daily experiences involve music in some form or other. We carry music around in phones. Birthday cards open to bursts of music, bought in shops into which music is pumped. If music were solid, it would clutter our city centres more com-prehensively than the discarded Domino's pizza boxes and empty clattering boxes of Monster energy drink we already find there.

Spotify, the MP3 player, streaming services all testify to the enormous value we place on music in our lives, while at the same time reduce music to a ubiquitous commodity. It's a mark, both of how hungry we are to listen and yet how willing we are to make the sounds we hear occur at our convenience, and around our personal circumstances. Again, we don't do this with any other art form. Imagine the Renaissance Popes demanded the construction of basilicas big enough to hold up ten thousand frescos. Then ordered them to be put on castors.

We make music omnipresent, yet incidental to our lives. Indeed, much of the music that passes us by has been specifically written as incidental music to the soundtrack of television and cinema. We turn an art form that seems wholly abstract into something specifically functional. We talk of mood music, and party music. Music to exercise to. We buy classical music in pre-packaged emotional categories: Smooth Classics to Cry To, the Nation's Best Bassoon Cadenzas for the Over-Forties, One Hundred Golden Baroque Moments for Cat Lovers.

We all have our favourite moments in music. The so-called 'shiver moments', when goosebumps form on the skin and the pulse suddenly quickens. The main theme at the start of Elgar's Cello Concerto. The rising choral climax at the end of Mahler's Resurrection Symphony. The vocal entry after the violin solo in the third of Strauss's *Four Last Songs*. These are some of mine, and you'll no doubt have your own. But think how un-thrilling these would be if we didn't work up to them. If we didn't experience these moments in the context of the rest of the pieces in which they come. If they were just bundled together in a quick capsule of Favourite Shiver Moments, all over in seconds. Would this quick fix be satisfying?

Not really. There's something rather sordid about sampling music in this way, as if we've broken into a sweet shop and eaten half a ton of fudge. Proper listening is also about recognising that work has to be done. That there's no short cut, no handy method of listening that'll allow you to derive the same amount of pleasure but in one fifth of the time. Those shiver moments have to be seen emerging within the whole piece; making sense of what's come before, and contributing to what happens after.

That's why I think we shouldn't shy away from music that's difficult. Difficulty requires concentration and application, but it's through these we come out of ourselves, and make ourselves – sometimes force ourselves – absorb another time, another rhythm, someone else's way of doing things. Opera, for example, can seem absurd, not least because it takes three or four hours. But when you stop thinking it's absurd to do nothing else but listen to opera for three or four hours, suddenly that world of sound you've given yourself over to starts making its own kind of sense.

Maybe we need to listen to music with a child's ear. Uncluttered with technical expressions and unencumbered by the need to compare this performance with earlier ones. I sometimes wonder that it's better I don't have a working knowledge of musical technique, because that would force me to find too many faults with what I've been listening to. When I hear the musically literate talk about a concert they've just attended, they often sound so miserable and dissatisfied; moping homewards lamenting the awkward glissandi, and the woodwind being perhaps a little too forceful on the lower register.

In the end, I know that I can't really explain why listening to music has the effect it does. Maybe it's because I work in comedy. I'm aware of the pitfalls in trying to explain something that's instinctive, rather than regulated. Anyone who tells me they're going to explain why something is funny, I know is going to sound like a pretentious and humourless idiot. Things are funny because they just are. It's amazing how easily you can destroy a joke by changing just one word or altering the sentence construction. There's a natural sense of rhythm, and timing, and colour to comedy that's very difficult to explain. I sometimes have very strange, abstract conversations with fellow comedy writers about basic things like numbers. Why certain numbers are funny, and others aren't. It used to be that, about twenty years ago, odd numbers were funnier than even ones. If you wanted a joke to end with a surprising number – 'How old was he then?' – you'd say, 'Forty-three'. Nowadays, for a strange, inexplicable reason, even numbers have become funnier. Especially ones ending in zeros. 'How old was he then?' 'Fifty.' Somehow, it seems funnier. Similarly with names. Forty years ago, Bill Fortescue-Willaby-Smithe would be considered a funny name. Nowadays, it just seems quaint. Today, a funny name would be something like Dirk Pig. Believe me, that's funnier. I can't explain why.

Comedy is a useful parallel, for me at any rate. It hints that our response to music might benefit from our being prepared to be a little bit more playful. Maybe listening again, this time like an open-eared child.

Shuffling towards a New Age

You'll see that I like to talk about music from the point of view of the listener. I don't mean listener in the sense of the consumer whose appetite drives the commercial CD and download market, but listener as a participant in the final musical experience. Daniel Barenboim's set of maverick but inspiring Reith Lectures celebrated the activity of listening. He pleaded for us to value the aural dimension in our culture as highly as we do the visual, and drew the distinction between the passive acceptance of music as background noise (hearing) and the active interpretation of music as inner experience (listening).

There are listening purists, of course, who insist we can only appreciate music in very fixed, clinical conditions (absolute silence in the house, or the rapt stillness of the concert hall). But with the advent of the MP3 and the iPod, we find ourselves listening to familiar and unfamiliar music in unexpected and disjointed ways. And perhaps it's high time we acknowledged that how we choose to listen can have a profound effect on how we understand the music we love.

I once jokingly wrote that, a hundred years from now, we'll

look back on all the advances in technology – new medicines, faster trains, more fuel-efficient cars – and declare that the one development that's brought most thrills to mankind is the shuffle function. For good or ill, electronically generated randomness is now one of the most popular ways of listening to music. After the historic sequence of Bronze Age, Renaissance, Industrial Revolution and Electronic Superhighway, we may now be entering the Shuffle Era.

Unexpected sequences can throw up illuminating comparisons. Take, for example, Bach and Ligeti – two very different composers, you might think. Yet it was only a chance segue from one to the other prompted by my shuffle function that made me see a connection I'd otherwise have missed, and one that's enhanced my listening pleasure of both of them. I've always enjoyed Ligeti's music, but have never been able to identify why. I have normally quite a timid relationship with most 'contemporary' music. I enjoy Berg, but Schoenberg less so. I can't seem to come to terms with Birtwistle and Boulez, but like Adès and Maxwell Davies, and have a particular fondness for Berio. There's no great scheme to all this. In the end, I've settled for the explanation that I just seem to like whoever produces the most interesting noises. I know it sounds the antithesis of any conventional appreciation of new music, but I can't find a better explanation.

As a child discovering classical music on Radio 3, I was always drawn to contemporary works that produced the most thrilling and unusual noises. Xenakis was particularly strange and alluring. But it's always been Ligeti who's grabbed my attention. His music seems both violent and humorous, with an aggressive drive, but always offering an inventive, playful exploration of the dynamics and range of the instruments. Without meaning in any way to sound derogatory, Ligeti's music has always seemed to me to sound childish, the sort of thrill and energy a child applies to an instrument such as the piano when they come across it for the first time – not afraid to bash it and stamp it or run their fingers right up to the highest note and all the way down to the lowest. It's a sudden relish bursting out for the first time, exploring a new world of amazing noises.

But it was only after one of Ligeti's piano studies shuffled on straight after a Bach prelude and fugue that it struck me why I'm drawn to the composer: it's for the same reason that I'm drawn to Bach. There are some people who say they need only listen to Bach; that he says everything that can be said musically. I take their point, in that Bach's music is often about music rather than himself. Each composition is an attempt to push the limits of the form that composition takes, or the instrument it's written for, whether it's a fugue or a solo cello suite, a concerto or a cantata. Bach's music, for me, is the music of someone relishing the possibilities of where music can go, of just how far he can take a theme, until breaking point (think of the *Musical Offering* and the *Art of Fugue*). It's not an abstract approach, but intensely solid and energetic. What it's not, though, is an attempt to write large his own personality.

I suddenly realised, thanks to my shuffle function, that this is precisely what Ligeti is doing: each composition is a fresh start, a wiping away of preconceptions about what the instrument or the form should sound like, and a fresh, childlike attempt to explore all the possibilities that lie ahead. That's how I listen to his music. And an enormous amount of pleasure it now gives me. Not bad for a random generator.

Falling on Deaf Ears

It's time, I think, to own up. There are bits of classical music that leave me cold. I know there'll be letters. Online message boards will start getting clogged up. But I've got to admit it: there are certain composers, or certain styles, or even certain moments within a larger piece I otherwise enjoy, where I can feel my mind wandering in a state of disconnection with the music. I just don't get Hindemith, try as hard as I can. (My publishers have now had to hire additional security.) I like Messiaen, but his *Turangalîla-Symphonie* leaves me clawing at the wall. (Death threats arrive from angry modernists.) Why have I recently warmed to Schumann but have always felt nonplussed by Mendelssohn? (I'm forced to go into hiding.) And, thirty years after becoming mesmerised by the music of Mahler, now's the time to admit that the middle movements of his symphonies, those fifteen-minute-long Ländler or simplistic children's songs, are still where my mind goes for a wander. (People start saying: hang on, he's got a point.)

Surely I'm not the only one to feel this? Not these specific examples: the music that leaves some of us intellectually or emotionally cold is the very same music that excites great feelings in others. I once told someone Hindemith did nothing for me, and he said he felt the same about Delius. I wanted to hit him. But we all, I'm sure, have our own particular pockets of numbness, where the music simply doesn't do anything for us.

It's an often isolating experience. If you're listening live at a concert and you slowly start to disengage from the performance, your eyes straying down to the programme notes and the adverts for luxury perfumes on the back, but then scanning across the audience, seeing them all in rapt attention, you suddenly feel a dunce. You look at the orchestra and you feel awkward that all that collective talent, all those years of childhood practice day after day and hard work at music college and impecunious slog for years holding down peripatetic teaching jobs, simply to be able to get to where they are now, here, in this fabulous orchestra, under the baton of this famed and famously temperamental conductor, is wasted on you because they're playing one of Mendelssohn's string symphonies.

My great failing is the Mass. No matter how great the musical genius behind it, the concert-hall Mass has just never inspired me. Even the fabulous, magnificent Bach, whose music I try to listen to every day – even his great and no doubt magnificent Mass in B minor has never moved me as much as, say, his cantatas or Passions. Maybe it's the shape of the thing. Again and again, composers' Masses start off punchily with the short, sharp *Kyrie* (the opening of Bruckner's Mass No. 2 is particularly mysterious) but then get bogged down in two great lumps of Latin theology in the *Gloria* and *Credo* that very few ever recover from. It's during these, as the skilled forces of chorus and orchestra try sounding impassioned about their affirmation that the incarnation of the Son was coterminous with the presence of the Father, that my attention falters. I can't help feeling that the composer would prefer to work with a more dramatic text (perhaps that's why requiems seem to have more impact, and are bigger box office; they dramatise a profoundly human story). Or the composer really has to believe fervently in the theological intricacies of what he's expressing (maybe, again, that's why Mass settings from the Renaissance and pre-Renaissance period seem more heartfelt, since they were such an accepted part of the daily ritual of worship, when religion was more central to a composer's life).

I think there's no shame in admitting to these blind spots. After all, why should we hold classical music up as an art form that is consistently brilliant? No one says, 'I absolutely love all painting,' or 'For me, there's nothing to beat any novel,' so why should we be expected to adore everything that's labelled 'classical music'? Likes and dislikes emerge. The vitriolic split between Brahms and Wagner supporters in the mid-nineteenth century was critical gang warfare as hostile as any mods-and-rockers beach fight in the 1960s: people seeing no merit in music other people passionately believed in. Thankfully, things aren't so destructive now; but, in defiance of those who criticise classical music against charges of, say, elitism or intellectual exclusiveness, have we perhaps not gone the other way and made it too perfect, too unchallengeable, too much beyond the whims of those who listen to it and who simply, being human, find in it things they love and things they don't?

Coffee and Surprises

My day tends to be ordered without surprises. Since I spend quite a bit of time writing, I work on my own for large chunks of the year and, when I do, I find I can write only with music on. And there's a pattern to the music I play. Usually Bach to start with, possibly to persuade my mind that, though it's first thing in the morning, my brain really is remarkably active. By eleven o'clock, I realise it's not, and so put on something a lot chewier, a big symphony or some piece that pulls all the stops out to make me properly wake up. *Gurrelieder* and coffee: that sort of thing. In the afternoon chamber music seems to fit the bill; by then my mind's telling me that, though I may think I'm winding down, I actually now need to focus. A lot.

So this is the listening pattern that typifies my day. Except it frequently falls apart when I stumble across a piece of music that quietly grows on me unawares, and which I find myself playing repeatedly, to the exclusion of everything else. These pieces are seldom 'greats', all-time classic favourites that have two dozen interpretations on CD, or the most celebrated of that composer's works. But there's something about them that I find illuminating. The two most recent

pieces to have had this effect on me are Thomas Tallis's motet
Salve intemerata and Stravinsky's Symphony in C.

The Tallis was written when the composer was a young
man, in the early 1530s, and, at around twenty-three minutes,
is possibly the longest single vocal movement of the sixteenth
century. This may sound an ambitious, youthfully arrogant
undertaking, but actually what impresses is how still and
deceptively unelaborate the piece is. It's a brave work, not
because it's complex but because it requires so much temporal space: it needs time to unfold, steadily growing, like
a work by Arvo Pärt but somehow richer, more mysterious.
The themes are long but utterly beautiful and the listener is
quietly draw into a slowed-down sense of time, a beating
heart, alive, yet demanding rapt attention to hear every beat.

Tallis went on to write more profound and ambitious
works in a career that survived the ecclesiastical shifts
between Catholic and Protestant reigns over England but
it's here in the opening moments of *Salve intemerata* that you
get a sense of who Thomas Tallis truly is and what at heart
he wants to write, unimpeded as yet by the demands of
competing theologies. It's these opening moments that captivated me when I first heard them and which held me still
for twenty-three minutes before I knew it.

Currently I find myself playing over and over again
Stravinsky's Symphony in C. Stravinsky has always seemed
to me to be one of those composers whom people admire
greatly rather than really love. Recently BBC Radio 3 perhaps
cruelly juxtaposed all his music with that of Tchaikovsky; the
message board was jammed with lovers of late Romanticism
expressing their annoyance that their enjoyment had to be
punctuated with Stravinsky's twentieth-century experiments.
I found it an interesting contrast; what impressed with the

Tchaikovsky was how masterfully he wrote and orchestrated traditional forms – raising the quality threshold, as it were, for popular musical genres such as the overture, the concerto or ballet – whereas with Stravinsky one was overwhelmed by the sheer breadth of his curiosity, his enthusiasm for picking up any genre and style and turning it inside out, teasing it to breaking point, absorbing lost elements of the past or pointing music towards a radically different future.

We normally think of Stravinsky as serious, but it was after hearing the Symphony in C that I started seeing him as someone who plays with music. It took me a while to work out why. It has a mysterious draw: it seems superficially a simple homage to the classic symphonic style of, say, Haydn. It's about the same length, and in the traditional pattern of four short, punchy movements, but this is no pastiche. Though there are nods towards traditional music elements like fugues and sonata form, and even minuet in some of the short dancelike themes, there's actually nothing in it that doesn't sound modern. It's as if two symphonies, one written several hundred years ago and one written in 1930, had simply been composed simultaneously.

There is so much play and invention in the Symphony in C, so much energy and variety built out of his short, simple themes, I never really want it to stop. But when it does, it does so with an ending that's thoroughly up-to-date and open; a succession of quiet, mysterious chords that raise more questions than they resolve and point to the route Stravinsky took in his later works. That's why, strangely enough, it's the Symphony in C, that most traditionally titled of all Stravinsky's works, that has provided me with the best way in to appreciating his more convention-defying works. And it's why I'm no longer surprised that the most unassuming pieces of music can end up being the most enlightening.

Making the Grade

I've always been a passionate listener of classical music. I stress 'listener', because I missed out on the opportunity to learn to read music or to take up an instrument. I did try the clarinet in the Sixth Form. The teacher was mostly morose and sarcastic, and all I remember from the weekly half-hour lessons was me making faces at him behind his back. After about six months of lonely gurning, I put my clarinet away and settled into the happy life of the listener.

From about the age of eleven, I'd been absolutely mesmerised by the sounds classical music could make. I liked to put Shostakovich on full blast on my brother's very expensive speakers. Sibelius, Stravinsky, Mahler bellowed out loud enough to annoy the neighbours. Bartók and Bach made the ceiling shake. I loved listening, and for quite some time came to accept that it was possible to go through life loving music but without the slightest idea how it was written or played. Yes, I felt occasionally excluded when a Radio 3 presenter talked about 'legato' or the second theme's playful transition to the major. On the whole, though, listening was the happy limit of my contact with music.

Then, for my fortieth birthday, my wife bought me a piano. Nothing too ambitious, but a good digital keyboard that gave the perfect sonic imitation of a baby grand. A thousand and one other buttons let it imitate everything else, from a small pipe organ to a steam train passing through Middlesbrough, but the piano setting remained on and I made a commitment to myself that I'd learn to play.

A year later, there I was sitting in someone's kitchen with a lot of seven-year-olds, clutching some sheet music. I was about to take my Grade 1 exam. Music exams, I found out, tend to take place in people's houses. Grade 1s tend to be sat by seven year olds, which is why I was in among a row of them, sitting on a very low plastic blue chair. Next door were the sounds of someone very, very competently playing an elaborate piece of Debussy. The music stopped, and out walked a six-year-old. A very tall person came over to me. She was probably only five feet five inches high, but from where I was sitting she seemed to touch the ceiling. 'Are you the candidate?' she said to me. Yes I was, I replied. 'Well then, good for you!'

I still wasn't due to play for another twenty minutes. Two other candidates were before me. One looked about four and sounded like she was able to play piano duets on her own, and the other was a remarkably precocious baby. While I waited, I had the chance to practise. There was a plastic toy keyboard for me to warm up on. It had red and yellow and green and blue keys, and made the noise of the instrument nursery teachers use when they accompany you all singing 'The wheels on the bus go round and round'. A sort of warm clanging sound. I clanged away, trying to prop my prepared piece up on a non-existent music stand.

It struck me then that I really didn't have to be here. I

could have run away, and no one would have been able to do anything about it. The police wouldn't go looking for me. A teacher wouldn't report me for unauthorised absence. I was forty-one. I'd been to the BAFTAs, directed television shows, made speeches in front of MPs and industry executives, once, on camera, duped O. J. Simpson into signing a piece of paper saying 'I Did It'. In 1997 I presented a three-hour live comedy election-night special. I'd even given the odd Radio 3 interval talk. I was a fully grown human being: I really didn't have to be in this peculiar situation in a stranger's kitchen.

Somehow, the knowledge that, on paper, this needn't be happening got me through. I was able to cope with the very weirdness of it all because it was entirely voluntary. Knowing that at any second I could run off into the suburbs was what made me stay. Also, my memory of swimming lessons.

These take me back a further six years. I could always swim, but never competently. I could save myself in an emergency, but would probably cause fatalities around me. Then, when I was in my mid-thirties, I saw a poster for 'Improvers' Lessons' at the local pool and signed up. A few days later, I was in the pool with a lot of middle-aged people used to running their own businesses, telling people what to do or generally having some control over their lives. These same people were now bobbing semi-naked in front of strangers, now being told what to do by someone in their twenties with a whistle. During a lesson on the crawl, one large middle-aged man shouted, 'Aerodynamically this just isn't possible!' and got out of the pool and never came back.

Sitting in the kitchen, clanging my Grade 1 prepared pieces out to a benchful of seven-year-olds, I resolved not to be a wet quitter. I'm glad I did. Learning the piano suddenly made music physical. I could touch music, not just listen to it. I could see it too. I can't say the music I made was anything someone else would want to hear, but it made me examine it close up. Suddenly, pieces I'd always loved were there in front of me, and what I saw was revelatory and disarming. The aria at the opening of Bach's *Goldberg Variations*, for example, now looked so simple, so direct. Frankly, there weren't that many blobs on the page.

Surprisingly, I wasn't disappointed. I think that seeing it all laid out and looking so simple only made it all the more magical. I found that was the case with all the pieces I played. The best of them were the ones that didn't try too many tricks, and where the composer had confidence in simplicity over complexity. Haydn does that a lot, I found. The variety and flourishes in his music are actually subtle nudges from a steady line or a forward pulse that doesn't go away. Of course, these were Grade 1 pieces, so nothing was going to be as taxing as Liszt's most flamboyant *Transcendental Studies*. And there was a downside: since Grade 1 is attempted mostly by young children, I did start off spending hours practising tunes from kids' music books, such as 'Farmer Joe's Billy Goat Got Stuck in a Bush', or whatever one of the hundreds of farmyard incidents children's music seems determined to celebrate in song. Worse than that, I had to play faux jazz. But once I'd got past 'Dental-Ache Blues' and 'Swinging Nanny', it wasn't too long before I could attempt Bach and Mozart.

Take heart: I'm told now that there are decent adult beginners' books, reflecting the expanding market for grown-ups taking up the piano. Today it's easier than ever before to practise. YouTube clips and online classes mean you can search out and focus on the individual pieces you like. Qualified piano teachers are more prepared to take on older pupils. If you've ever yearned to make that leap from listener to practitioner, there's never been a better time.

We will all have our own different reasons for wanting to play, and different ways of making ourselves practise. In my case, it was straightforward; I'm so used to living by deadlines, I knew the only way I was going to push myself was by imposing them on me, through weekly piano lessons with a teacher and a Grade 1 exam applied for and placed firmly in my schedule. Which is how I found myself in a stranger's kitchen, warming up on a blue plastic chair. Soon I was called in, and set myself up at the owner's rather impressive grand piano.

A word of advice to anyone taking Grade 1: find out what type of piano you're going to be doing the exam on, and make sure you practise on something similar. I hadn't touched a grand piano before. The keys on my digital were very light, while those on this monster were so heavy it felt like I suddenly had to improvise on a new instrument. I might as well have been playing the trombone. It was so ridiculous – indeed, everything connected with this occasion seemed so loopy – that I laughed all the way through my prepared piece. I passed, though. It really is that easy. So you have no excuse.

drunk next to her was possibly the UK equivalent of finding yourself standing next to Wonder Woman.

I was similarly usurped by a pleasant surprise last month when I was directing a feature film. Directing a film is normally something one should get very excited about. Not a lot of people get to do it, everyone treats you like you're important, and you get to boss actors around and tell them to do anything you want. It's an astonishing ego trip, and I wouldn't recommend it to anyone who has the slightest psychotic tendencies. But it was fun. I was filming a political comedy and, for budget reasons, the scenes set at the UN in New York were being filmed inside the Royal Festival Hall in London. Which is where, while I was meant to be concentrating on directing an enormous crowd scene recreating the UN Security Council preparing for a major vote authorising international military action, I was instead popping through an unattended door that led into the concert hall itself. There Krystian Zimerman was rehearsing on his own all afternoon. Standing listening to a piano master playing a Bach partita seemed much more important than anything else, and for a brief moment film-making seemed like a lot of expensive buffoonery. Eventually I got my act together and left the hall to go back to the day job. Filming was fun and fulfilling, but my memory of that day will always be of the man at the piano.

It reminded me of a similar stumble about ten years ago when, for my sins, I found myself hosting a telecom conference in Birmingham. It was at the newly opened Birmingham Symphony Hall and, during a toilet break, I went through the wrong door and turned up in the upper circle of the concert hall itself as Simon Rattle was rehearsing the CBSO and Chorus in John Adams's *Harmonium*. I found myself the only other person in the hall and got treated to a performance of the whole piece before I suddenly remembered I was meant to be next door, introducing a thousand businesspeople to the UK's leading telephone marketing strategist. That day job was less fun than the filming.

I love stumbling upon music. Especially when the music catches you unawares, but so completely that all your other priorities are dumped for a moment. I first got to know Bruckner in the early 1980s when there was a trend for playing it in the background of TV space documentaries. Hearing it for the first time, the music seemed much more interesting than anything the presenter was saying or any of the wonders of the Universe his team of computer graphicists were simulating.

We can easily complain today that music is so omnipresent, blasted out of the corner of every room or public building we stagger into. But that at least gives us the increased possibility we might happen upon something unexpected or new. Wandering into a church at lunchtime in a busy city and hearing someone practising the organ. Going for a walk and overhearing a piece playing loudly on someone's home system through an open window. That's how, when I was an undergraduate still working out what his attitude to classical music was, I found myself rooted to the spot absolutely mesmerised by the sound of Strauss's *Four Last Songs* drifting out of a student's open window. I'd never heard such unashamed but sincere romanticism before and it had me frozen to the floor.

These unexpected surprises remind me of music's unique ability to come at you like an overheard conversation. Such moments leave you speechless and still; neither do you want the moment to pass nor the time of day to start up again. They're reminders of what one must never take for granted.

Classicool

I thought of beginning with a deliberately provocative opener along the lines of, 'Why is classical music much, much better than rock and pop?', but backed down. There's too raw, too arrogant a claim behind that question; it presumes different genres of music can be graded into absolute and fixed quantities. As if pop is worse than jazz, but jazz is one up from folk, for example. As if, more particularly, the finest songs of Bob Dylan or the Beatles are of less merit than the juvenilia of Hugo Wolf.

I'm always wary of any universal claims made by a critic, and have been ever since as an English Literature student I read the opening line of the renowned critic F. R. Leavis's influential work, *The Great Tradition*. It reads: 'The great English novelists are Jane Austen, George Eliot, Henry James and Joseph Conrad.' There are so many questions to be asked here (like, for example, 'Where's Charles Dickens?' and 'How is Henry James English when James Joyce isn't?') that Leavis's claim to certainty immediately founders and you're left challenging the judgement of those who decided he was eminent in the first place.

No, a healthy suspicion of any absolutist proclamations is probably a good thing. But I raised the comparison with rock and pop because I wanted to get to grips with what it is that makes classical music so special. So special to me, that is. Like any religious believer, no matter how ecumenical their openness to other faiths, there has to sit inside a residual belief in the rightness of their faith over others. Like any citizen, there has to be a latent loyalty to their own country above any fondness for another. Yes, we know these emotional links are possibly irrational, but there they are just the same. So, for me, classical music seems more valid, more enriching and satisfying than any other form of music, despite all I've carefully thought through and written down in the two paragraphs above.

So now I have to ask myself: why? Why, if the house caught fire and I had only five seconds to grab some CDs, would they all be classical music ones? Maybe it's something to do with context. Popular music seems so much rooted in context – when it's recorded, where you first heard it – that a lot of its energy and power relies on it being the sound of a particular moment in time. The fact that we can easily date most tracks to a particular period ('that sounds so early nineties') indicates how rooted in fashion this music is.

I know I'm being hugely simplistic, but it does seem to me that both the strength and the limits of popular music rest on its being part of a cultural trend (even if it's setting that trend) so that once fashion has moved on, once time has passed, it can very quickly appear dated.

Then, of course, we listen to certain artists because they bring back memories. Aged fifty, we may pull out a CD we bought when we were twenty because we want to be reminded of what we were doing and thinking when we were that age. Who we were going out with, where we lived, who we went to that stadium concert with. The bulk of us start listening to popular music as teenagers and our favourites as we grow older stay mostly those from that time. Hence Billy Joel concerts are full of fifty-five-year-olds and Blur ones full of people in their forties.

With classical music I have no sense of time, of historic moment, being a limiting factor. I find it miraculous that I've been listening to, say, Mahler's Ninth Symphony for nearly forty years and I'm still discovering fresh things about it. But none of my new thoughts concern my time as a teenager. I'm listening to it not to bring back memories, but to discover something new. I'm not trying to recreate the moment I first heard it; I'm trying to create a fresh moment of hearing something original in it for the first time. Similarly, after forty years of listening to classical music, I'm uncovering fresh surprises, discovering new composers, but again thoughts of historic time don't come into it. It's only in the past few years I've come to listen to and love Schumann. And the references to Victoria and Tallis elsewhere in this book might indicate that Renaissance and early-Baroque choral music is a particular obsession at the moment.

That's what seems so magical about classical music. It's such a vast space, a lifetime of exploration still wouldn't seem enough. Popular music is very much of the moment; classical music demands an eternity.

Surprisingly Ugly

Do you like ugly music? There are those who would say all modern music is ugly now, and classical music has always been punctuated with extremely fraught arguments among composers and musical theorists about whether music is there just to be beautiful, or if occasional bursts of ugliness are an occasional fall-out from its need to be consistently innovative and challenging. What first attracted me to the music was not just the beauty of the best of melodies or the power of a large-scale composition, but of captivating and unusual and, yes, ugly sounds that could be produced by the likes of Xenakis or Ligeti or Messiaen. Not knowing anything about theory, I was unaware of what conventions were being overturned. The noises these people were making were just interesting.

Which isn't to say I like them all. I still haven't found anything to keep me listening to Harrison Birtwistle, no matter how hard people urge me to try. Perhaps this says more about me than it does about Birtwistle's music, but it does raise the questions: how are we to evaluate music that seeks to liberate itself from preconceived judgement and expectations? How can you tell good challenging music from bad?

In a period of universal experimentation, when will someone publish the final results of those experiments?

Perhaps I was taking the wrong tack by asking if you enjoy ugly music. Are you meant always to enjoy music? Does one enjoy a well-written book about the Holocaust, do you enjoy looking at a Jackson Pollock, are you meant to enjoy a film about political corruption, do people enjoy *King Lear*, does the nation enjoy watching its national football team getting beaten? We are perfectly willing to approach other art forms and media with an expectation that we will not necessarily be totally happy and uplifted by what we experience; that sometimes we benefit from a little hard work or from a confrontation with something challenging. So why can't we be open to this possibility in music?

Composers do sit down to write deliberately alienating, ugly sounds: the brutal dissonant chords that slice into Mahler's Tenth Symphony, Ives's playful cacophony of different marching bands in *Three Places in New England*. One senses the composers knew what they were up to, and anticipated the ugliness of the resultant noise. That was ugliness designed to get a specific reaction, and ugliness set in a wider musical landscape.

One of the ugliest pieces of music I've come across is Prokofiev's Second Symphony. He wrote it almost out of a jealous pique at all the attention Stravinsky was getting after *The Rite of Spring* and, following on from the more conventional melodies and rhythms of the *Classical* Symphony, the composer deliberately sat down to write music of 'iron and steel' that would get him noticed. I find it pretty unbearable; a deliberate grinding clank of industrial noise that shows no sign of letting up before it reaches the end (and good luck to anyone who manages to get to the end).

Years later, Prokofiev confessed that he was never entirely sure what he was meant to be doing in the Second Symphony, a confession that reassures people like me who sometimes feel like we're meant to thoroughly appreciate every piece of challenging music ever served up to us.

In the end, I suppose, ugliness is in the eye of the beholder. Stravinsky's *The Rake's Progress* was greeted with a cry of 'What ugliness!' from the radical young Pierre Boulez when it was premiered in 1951. I found Boulez's comment in Alex Ross's splendid history of twentieth-century classical music, *The Rest is Noise*, and one of the delights of the book is the hilarious account of how so desperately avant-garde the avant-garde got in the 1950s and '60s that they began to reject not just romantics, traditionalists and melodists, but each other.

Boulez seems the most hilariously unhappy, labelling Cage's gimmicks with prepared pianos as fascist and spouting out a bile-ridden obituary on Schoenberg the week he died, berating the godfather of serialism for not going far enough in revolutionising rhythm and form as well as harmony. 'I do not hesitate to write, not out of any desire to provoke a stupid scandal, but equally without bashful hypocrisy and pointless melancholy: SCHOENBERG IS DEAD.' It's a laughable obduracy, and a wonderful illustration of the paradox of demanding creative liberty while passing immutable judgement.

After reading this, I listened to some Boulez and though I certainly didn't find it ugly, I did find it rather dull. Schoenberg's music I still find much more interesting. Not necessarily enjoyable, but interesting none the less.

No matter: Boulez sounds thick-skinned enough not to mind my opinion. Maybe I would have enjoyed him more if his music had been uglier. Boulez is dead now, of course.

Hear Me Out

A speech I gave to the Royal Philharmonic Society, spoken to a room full of conductors, composers, musicians and other people far more secure about the topic than me but who were all happy to listen.

I can't sing, can't even whistle, and, until recently, couldn't really say I played an instrument. That last omission officially changed when I received a certificate that said I'd managed to persuade a professional in the room for ten minutes that I had a tiny grasp of the piano, and had passed my Grade 1. I realise that, of course, when it comes to music it doesn't matter how much or how little technical expertise one has. It doesn't matter if the sum total of your involvement in music is just as a listener, for music transcends any limits on ability, nationality, religion, or language. It is the most magical act of communication.

That word, communication, is what I want to discuss: how we – what I'll call the artistic community – communicate with our audience, and how much we let them communicate with us. I'll concentrate on music, but my thoughts take in the arts generally. I choose music, because, despite my lack of technical expertise, it is the artistic experience I'm most happy with.

Classical music has been, for me, the single most inspiring, most moving, most magical thread running through my whole cultural experience. It's the art form in whose presence I feel most comfortable, most myself. And it's probably no accident that when I first embarked on a career in comedy I did it as a producer on radio, playing with sound.

I can trace my love of classical music from the moment, aged eleven, I attended my first musical appreciation lesson and the needle of a badly battered record player dropped with a loud thump onto a scratchy recording of Holst's *The Planets*. Then I heard sounds that excited me in a way that somehow the recordings of King Crimson and David Bowie never did at the time.

So began my musical career, as a listener. I soon took advantage of a newly opened public library only yards down the road to join their fantastically new and extensive record section. And I eagerly ate up Beethoven, Mahler, then Sibelius, Shostakovich, Bach's amazing *St Matthew Passion*, the eccentricities of Berlioz, the purity of Bruckner, the invention of Nielsen. Discovering Radio 3, my encounters expanded. I heard a season of Rubbra symphonies in the early 1980s and have loved his symphonies ever since. I discovered Bartók, Walton, and strange noises, such as Xenakis.

I loved strange noises. I had no notion of what was considered contemporary or old-fashioned, cutting edge or period. It was all wonderful and new. I wasn't scared of the avant-garde because I had no notion of what an avant-garde was.

I realised this a few years ago, taking my son to school. He was eight or nine at the time. A piece of Ligeti was on the radio. Not to put him off with what maybe he would think was a strange, slightly disturbing noise, I tried to draw a simple analogy. 'Sounds a bit like bees buzzing, doesn't it?' I said. He listened for a bit, then said, 'No, it sounds like a lot of penguins fighting for a fish, and one of them's just got it.'

He was right – that's precisely what it sounded like. He was listening much harder than me. And it struck me then that I was worrying about my son being put off classical music by being exposed to something that may have been too difficult.

And that worrying was unnecessary, because labelling the music difficult was a very adult way of categorising it in the first place. He, not knowing much about chromaticism, harmony or serialism, nor anything about theory, had no reason to label what he was hearing as being significantly different from, say, Handel. It was just a very interesting, very alluring, piece of ordered sound. So too, when I first heard Rubbra, was I unaware that his music, along with the music of many English symphonists of the 1950s, 1960s and 1970s, had been critically banished from the airwaves and concert halls because they were deemed embarrassingly traditional. So I had no idea I wasn't meant to like it.

Listening to classical music is a journey, not a state; an activity, not a meditation. Music is not a background noise. It's something you bring into the foreground of your experience, by engaging with it, by doing some work. Only recently have I come to listen properly to Schumann, Haydn and, especially, Bach, and begun to get that sense of rich, deep satisfaction that I encountered more immediately, as an adolescent, in Mahler. I'm aware that it's easy to fall back on quasi-mystical, pretentious language when trying to talk about one's experience of classical music, but that shouldn't stop us trying. We don't talk about music enough.

As someone who's never felt he's had the technical language at his fingertips, I feel all I can do is talk about it in whatever English I have at my command. I want to emote about how I feel. After a concert, I want to grab people by the lapels and tell them how lucky we are as a species that, out of all the hundreds of billions of us who ever lived, one of us managed to come up with the *Goldberg Variations*. But I don't, because that's not the done thing. So instead I mention that the café downstairs does some fabulous flapjacks.

There's no way anyone is ever going to fully 'know' music, but I do think there's an obligation to allow as many people as possible to know as much about it as they can. That's not the same as saying that music could become more accessible through marketing gimmicks. I'm always suspicious of any concert that puts other things in the way of the music – fireworks, laser displays – as if scared that the music by itself will not be enough.

Nor does it mean the classical music industry has to start talking awkwardly in the language of the street, going on about how Beethoven was a crazy guy, and Wagner made action movies. Or getting Jamie Oliver to talk about Buxtehude. It's not that at all. But it is about developing a language that talks to the audience, aware of their intelligence and appetite, but also recognising that they will have questions that need answering.

It was when I first started going to concerts I realised that seeing a piece of music performed live was the best single explanation of what it was about. It didn't need words or footnotes. My fondest musical memories are of live concerts, of seeing and hearing *Belshazzar's Feast* for the first time at a Glasgow prom, and being overwhelmed by the violence and energy of Walton's music. Of seeing what *The Rite of*

Spring looked like, not just what it sounded like. But outside the concert hall I feel there is a greater and greater appetite for verbal communication about music. As traditional music teaching in schools diminishes, the language is taken away, but the feeling is still there. People want to have proper grown-up conversations about why music matters, about why the arts matter.

That's why I think it's necessary to have an emotional debate about music as well as an intellectual one. Music is a dialogue between the heart and the head. Too often, though, a review will concentrate on how well a piece is played, but not on why that piece deserves to be played in the first place.

We need to wake up to the fact that people are now asking basic questions. Why are we musical? Why did people write symphonies? Why do we have the string quartet? They seem childlike, these questions, but they're there to provide us with the opportunity to enthuse and explain and demonstrate the answers we first stumbled upon in our musical journey and which encouraged us to make that journey in the first place. Figure out our answers to those questions, and it will help us tackle some more simple, yet more terrifying, questions. Why should the state spend money on the arts? Why do we have opera and why is it so expensive? Why should we have so many orchestras in London?

Just as I think any performer tries to perform music as if for the first time, with all that energy and excitement that comes from discovering a new piece – maybe trying to recreate the memory of falling in love with a piece when first hearing it as a child – and just as people regularly say of a brilliant conductor that they seem to conduct as if recreating the energy an audience must have felt when the piece was first played decades, even centuries, before, so too I think we need to communicate our knowledge with the passion we first encountered as children.

I can't believe I'm about to say this, but I find I can't listen to Mozart. I don't dislike him, I'm just unmoved by him. I realise I'm in a minority and I'm intrigued as to why this is. I broadcast a Radio 3 interval talk about this a few months ago, and the controller, Roger Wright, rather mischievously scheduled it in the middle of a live relay of *The Marriage of Figaro*. I received the biggest response to anything I've ever done. Buckets of letters and emails. None of them hostile. One or two confessing they agreed with me. But many more patiently, movingly, explaining why they loved Mozart.

I think we should at all times keep trying to ask and to answer the most basic of questions about music, about the arts. What are they there for?

For me, they're not there for any other reason than to remind us that, no matter where we are, whether we're learned, in prison, poor, successful, alone or average, our material circumstances are not all that we have, that we can see beyond ourselves, that we're human and are therefore dignified. That's my answer. I'm sure each of you has a different one. I just wish we all had more opportunities to express them.

The Big Tune

Listening to the opening of John Adams's *Shaker Loops* recently, I was struck by how little classical music concerns itself with tunes. We recognise tunes instantly – the start of Mendelssohn's Violin Concerto, the choral theme in Beethoven's Ninth – but we celebrate them all the more because actually the big, grand tune is quite rare. Beethoven's choral theme is memorable because there's nothing else as self-contained in the symphony; what other tunes there are seem more like shorter starting points for more interesting variation and development. The most famous piece of classical music, the opening of Beethoven's Fifth, is a motif rather than a tune.

Shaker Loops, the opening movement especially, is about rhythm, repeated patterns, pulse, a constant thrum of twittering, nervous, jagged little motifs on string instruments that go on to supply the energy and structure to the piece. You don't listen to *Shaker Loops* thinking, Where's the tune?, because there's clearly no need for one.

What this reminds me is that listening to a piece of music is more than a boiling down of it to its 'best bits', the memorable tunes and climaxes that go on to become the popular tracks on compilation albums. Cake is great, but a diet of just cake plays havoc on the digestive system and causes unspeakable misery further down the line.

The fact is that listening to music is not an instant activity, the work of a few minutes. Ever since composers took music away from the palace and the cathedral and placed it in the concert hall, music has demanded not only more attention but more time. Tunes, themes, motifs, phrases, call them what you will, start becoming characters in a drama greater than themselves and one that demands the time needed to perform it from start to finish.

Robert Simpson's Ninth Symphony, written in 1987, pushes this sense of a journey through time to breaking point, consisting of one fifty-minute movement, driven by a pulse and maintaining the same tempo throughout, defying the drama to emerge and form anything other than a 'tune.' Tense chords, shifting keys, bursting rhythms, loud brass climaxes: it's an exciting, nervous achievement.

Just as memorable as a good tune is where a composer places it. Sibelius's Second Symphony, for example, ends on a mighty good tune, but more interesting is the ending of his Fifth, written just thirteen or so years later, in 1915, where a glorious tune breaks out towards the end of the final movement and feels like the traditional basis for a stirring climax. But then, just as everything seems to resolve perfectly, the symphony stops abruptly with a succession of strange, isolated chords, as if the drama immediately preceding it is being swept away like a distraction. It's a very unnerving ending but, I think, a conscious recognition on the part of the composer of the kind of expectation we bring to a piece of music when it develops into a good tune.

The most intriguing manipulation of tune is, for me, by Tchaikovsky. In my disdainful adolescence, I tended to look down on his music as the flashy pot-boiling of a decent tunesmith, happy to throw in vulgar cannon-and-mortar effects to appeal to the crowds. Then the drama of *Romeo and Juliet* suddenly hit me; putting unforgettably beautiful tunes against each other to enact a very immediate tragedy of wasted lives whose union is broken. But the real revelation came when I first heard the Sixth Symphony and, in particular, its unbearable final movement. I say unbearable, because in that final movement Tchaikovsky does an extraordinarily brave thing as a composer; brave but, to the listener, extremely cruel. He gives us one of his greatest, most beautiful tunes, ravishing and sad, about two minutes into the movement and then, when we've heard it once and start anticipating what he's going to do with it next, he kills it. Dead. It's never heard again. There are subdued echoes at the end, but they're broken fragments; there's never again that moment of total rhapsody. It's like watching a charismatic character suddenly appear in the final act of a play and then almost immediately get shot. It's utterly heartbreaking; and memorable drama. It's for me one of the most disturbing portrayals of hopelessness in all music. All inspired by a mere tune.

Words into Music

Ho di ladyfact sun con brilliant de maximeltingly sensiness. A sequence of nonsense words. What did you make of them? Gibberish? Or did you like the sound? Some of the first classical music I listened to was sung in German. Texts from Mahler symphonies and songs, the words of the *St Matthew Passion*. But I didn't speak a word of German, so essentially I was listening to a kind of sung nonsense. I could, of course, follow the translation, and with the Bach I was familiar with each stage of the Passion narrative. But, still, I was listening rather than reading, hearing sounds rather than translating meaning. And I got rather to like the noise that sung German made.

With a Bach cantata I'm in more unfamiliar territory. What interest do I have in following the translation of a Lutheran chorale interspersed with hackwork theological verse written by a number of largely forgotten seventeenth-century sermonisers? And yet the music makes perfect sense. The words become an integral part of a sound that suggests hell, salvation, glory, resurrection, dejection, joy, anger, or any one of many hundreds of spiritual moods that Bach had to summon up for whatever Sunday of the year it happened to be.

So how important are the words for music? I ask the question because I'm now in the middle of writing a libretto for a comic opera. There's a conflict in my head between wanting the words to express as much as possible, while realising that they have to hold back and let the music take responsibility for expressing the true narrative of the piece. It's the music that's crucial; not the words. And yet the words will shape the music, so they have to justify the enormous amount of creative work that's going to be prompted by them.

Classical music is frequently caught in a tension; between its abstract nature – a sound that can't be seen, a noise that should mean nothing but will mean much – and the very physical, earthy nature of what music is, seeing people exert themselves in an orchestra or chamber recital, a conductor sweating, an opera performance only coming alive with the right staging, the perfect casting. This creative tension applies to words in music. On the one hand, whatever is being sung conveys precise meaning, while simultaneously the words, and their meanings, dissolve into a greater sound, a larger meaning, that can't really be translated into anything other than the finished piece of music. As one little example of how fragile this balance is, think of the many occasions when you've heard the most wonderful music in an opera and then read the translation into English and realised they're all singing about something mundane like opening a door. At times like these, you feel it's far better not to know.

And yet some of the greatest moments in music are purely verbal. Victoria's second Requiem, composed in 1603, is an astounding, cavernous sound. It's a continual source of amazement that in the *Kyrie* section, just six words, 'Kyrie eleison, Christe eleison, Kyrie eleison', can become three minutes of the most intense drama, the overwhelming vastness of the 'Kyries' a yearning for something superhuman and permanent, contrasted with the intimate, humble, human setting of the 'Christe'. It's an extraordinary span of sound, a three-act opera in three minutes. For an equally memorable but much more intimate emotional response to death, listen to the setting of 'I heard a voice from heaven' in Herbert Howells's Requiem. It's impossible not to be moved by this restrained yet devastating expression of personal grief.

The Norwegian composer Knut Nystedt has written a choral piece called *Immortal Bach*. It opens with Bach's chorale setting *Komm, süsser Tod* but suddenly slows down, each note of the original harmonic structure being prolonged for different durations simultaneously. For the remaining five minutes, then, the words in Bach's chorale dissolve into continuous sound divested of discrete meanings. It's a mesmerising but baffling effect; language is turned to pure noise and pulse becomes stillness. And yet the effect, for me, is to reinforce the beauty of the original Bach. Trying to freeze-dry a sound to make it seem permanent takes away the fleetingness, the life that made it special in the first place.

If we think of music as pure abstraction, then we have a lot more exceptions to the rule than we can cope with. The earliest recognised piece of secular Western music is a setting of words, the thirteenth-century roundelay *Sumer is icumen in*, while the greatest music of the next three hundred years was plainchant and choral polyphony, unaccompanied settings of words. Of all the musical instruments, the one we pay most money to hear, the one we derive most pleasure from playing, is the voice. It's a useful antidote to any mystical

The Museum of Lost Keyboards

Visitors to the museum are asked to wear one of our audio-headsets at all times otherwise they will become painfully confused. The man in the headset will quietly explain the exhibits then at full volume ask you to leave. This is a transcript of what he says.

Welcome, welcome, welcome. Welcome to the Museum of Lost Keyboards. The collection is owned by Sir Samuel Holt, chairman of Triple Helix Insurance, and himself a keen player of the onde martenot. We hope, when your visit is complete, you'll share Sir Samuel's belief that the sole purpose of man is music. And that the keyboard is as a ribcage to the soul.

We start our tour at the entrance to the first gallery. Here is perhaps the most valuable instrument in the collection: a 1754 piano made entirely from diamonds. It was commissioned by Prince Gregor Esterházy for his bride, who died from the shock of receiving it. It is made from twenty-nine thousand diamonds and is now very rarely played manually, since the sound is excruciating.

In 1944, the diamond piano was installed on the

fifty-fourth atrium of the Rockefeller Center in New York. Rockefeller was a poor player and adapted the instrument to play sheets of piano roll only he could afford, using parchment made from crushed and stiffened truffles.

Nestling alongside the diamond piano, on a tiny plinth, is Exhibit Two: Glenn Gould's two-inch spherical piano, made in 1963. The instrument was bought by Gould in 1961 as a full-size conventional Steinway grand. The Canadian perfectionist was immediately dissatisfied with the sound, and began removing some, and then all, of the keys. Troubled by the dimensions, he also sheared the instrument with a lathe, arriving at the more harmonious spherical shape it is now. Though the piano could now make no noise whatsoever, Gould professed himself delighted that at least it couldn't make the wrong noise.

To be fully comfortable while crouching down to play, Gould often shaved his legs. And wore no shoes, in the conventional sense of the word.

To your right is a harpsichord made from snow. It was first built in Stockholm in 1729, but melted two hours later. Using his original plans, its builder, T. M. Hofflefife, made a snow reconstruction within minutes, which he then placed on a suburban glacier to preserve it for summer recitals. The harpsichord is now kept at sub-zero temperatures on the top of a white column, towering twenty thousand feet above sea level. The sound is utterly delightful. But the low temperature makes it impossible to play, since most pianists' fingers stick to the keyboard, and frostbite ruins their careers for ever. There is a recording of Wanda Landowska playing Bach wearing mittens, but the playing is – for all Landowska's mastery of the Bach repertoire – singularly inept.

If the snow harpsichord is played at room temperature in

a concert hall, the player has just twenty minutes before it turns to water.

You will notice, as you wander through the first gallery, that it is completely dark. Although the museum's benefactor, Sir Samuel Holt, had perfect eyesight, he never used it, often working at night or under beds. And it was his express stipulation that his keyboards be displayed entirely in blackout, inspiring the visitor to listen more carefully and to think not of the tempting sweetmeats of be-lighted things. But remember that anyone who falls over an instrument will be fined and possibly interrogated.

I will be quiet for thirty seconds while you walk over there to where I'm pointing.

Here now is our second gallery, which houses living and extinct instruments. All that's left of the piano-shaped creature on your right are its bone pedals and strings, here preserved in a jar of formaldehyde. It's thought that the Pianogator lived fourteen thousand years ago on Easter Island, where fossilised keyboards have been retrieved from the shoreline. Paleomusicologists think that the creature's two extended forelimbs allowed it to play itself, curling the limbs under its belly to pluck a row of black and white nipples.

Next to the exhibit is a bucket of piano milk. Be careful.

On the western wing of this gallery is an overhead photograph and working model of a naturally occurring piano found in the forests of Sri Lanka. This phenomenon is very rare, and only happens when a row of forty-four elephants form an exact straight line, their tusks becoming a neat row of ivory keys eight hundred metres long. The elephant line-up has to take place backing up onto a teak forest so overgrown that the branches and leaves act as an enclosed chamber, magnifying the sound that would be made by the elephants if anything dropped on their tusks from a great height. The only known instance of this was in 1893, when just such an arrangement of elephants was hit by a meteor, creating what many local witnesses said was the best sound ever.

Please move on now. If there were any light, the visitor would notice the walls are decorated with pastel drawings of the very last clavichord being hunted by dogs. Sir Samuel is glad this type of butchery now can't be seen by the naked eye.

We move into the chamber of pioneer keyboards. The first instrument is this fine example of a 1952 Westinghouse Nutronium, the world's first nuclear forte piano. The Westinghouse's keyboard and pedals are a standard size, while the main body of the forte piano houses a nuclear generator. The player strikes keys manually, which in turn causes a set of hammers to hit the strings, each hammer being launched by a small nuclear device. Pedals allow the player to control the half-life of each explosion. The Nutronium on display here was tested in the Nevada desert by Michelangeli.

Moving round to the small antechamber at the back, the visitor comes upon Sir Samuel Holt's most prized possession. It's the 1941 Broadman piano, owned by Stalin. Stalin was a keen music lover, and adapted this piano so the keys sent pulses of electricity along wires connected to the open brains of members of the bourgeoisie, causing them to scream, tunefully, in pain. Stalin would often stay up late to hear screams organised in rhythmic patterns devised by the Soviet Union's greatest composers. Shostakovich once wrote that 'my Sonata for Howling Agitators, though not without artistic merit, is perhaps the most shameful thing I've ever done'. It is Sir Samuel's contention that music transcends the basis of context. Even when screamed out, as here, by actual left-wing volunteers, it is still inexplicably beautiful.

The visitors will notice, as they leave this gallery, that they are gradually coming round to Sir Samuel's point of view. Move now.

We arrive at the largest keyboard instrument in the collection: an organ built from cathedrals. It is thought that thirty-four cathedrals from southern France were reconfigured, brick by brick, to make this majestic vaulted specimen. The organ took five centuries to construct, at a cost of fifteen thousand lives and the complete economic ruin of south-western Europe. A small school for trainee choristers has been housed in one of its pipes since 1849. The sound of the orchestra is very beautiful, not unlike a squadron of angels refuelling in a church while in a good mood.

As we enter the end of the next room, you will notice a life-sized model of the ZZ300 Speakodreft, the first piano to be sent into space. The instrument comes equipped with a piano roll mimicking mankind's most representative sound: a mixture of desire and regret counterpointed with helplessness.

We now enter the room of smart keyboards, starting with an early example of a forte piano that only plays when you've got something to hide. It was built by the great Alpheus Babcock in 1814. Babcock was determined to perfect his instruments, and in the early 1800s made keys so precisely weighted, shaped, crafted and balanced they became powerfully sensitive to the slightest variations in touch. Even to the small, almost imperceptible changes in heart rate and blood pressure brought on by the keeping of a closely guarded secret. So anyone playing at Babcock unwittingly let on whether he was concealing inner thoughts and fears. This model was very popular in the drawing rooms of Regency England, though it led to the breakdown of many aristocratic marriages. It is used today to extract information from the inmates of Guantánamo Bay.

Babcock's smart pianos were further modified in the early 1900s to become touch-sensitive to specific emotional states. A good example of this is the 1934 Stood Clarisizor, the first electronic keyboard to know when its player was wasting its time. The Clarisizor calculates the technical ability of a player from any sweat he deposits when opening the lid. The instrument will then only play phrases it knows will be played well, and declines to play anything it believes will be below the musical standard it considers acceptable.

Come. In this room you will see the only known example of a self-perpetuating fugue. The fugue has at least one hundred and fifty parts and has been going since 1687. It may never end. No one knows who composed it, though it has trace elements of Bach, Debussy, Ligeti and Haydn. Over a hundred generations have performed in the fugue and the instrument on which it is being played has been repaired so many times its entire structure is completely different from the one in which it started. The fugue itself is said by experts to have no musical merit whatsoever.

And now ... we come to the final keyboard in the exhibition, and the only one to be illuminated. It's the 1704 Bossendorfer Anity, generally considered to be the most perfect piano in the world. Fifteen major land battles have been fought over the Bossendorfer, which was finally brought to Paris by Napoleon after the sacking of Vienna in 1809. It was said the French emperor fell in love with it so much it distracted him from the planning of his Russian campaign in 1812. Rumour has it the sound of the Bossendorfer is so wonderful that anyone listening will find all further sensory experience disappointing and unnecessary. Normally players now only play memories of the sound, and listeners listen only to the echoes.

It may interest the visitor to know that Napoleon spent most of his days in exile on the island of Saint Helena plotting to get back to the Bossendorfer. He made hundreds of tunnel diagrams with his blood.

Exit from the museum is forbidden to those who do not sit and play this keyboard. Play now, then leave for the streets and do not come back again.

Who the Hell was Malcolm Arnold?

The death of Malcolm Arnold in 2006 produced many printed testimonies to his originality and genius as a composer for the orchestra. Instrumentalists in particular remarked on the pleasure playing his pieces gave them. But one word recurred throughout those obituaries, and that was *anger*. Many people who knew and loved Arnold's music have expressed tremendous anger at how underrated he was within the wider critical community; that by writing tunes, deflating excess gravitas with humour and achieving popular appeal, Malcolm Arnold has somehow surrendered his right to be considered a proper, 'serious' composer. In particular, the testimonies to him speak of how unjustly neglected his cycle of nine symphonies is.

I've written before of what a remarkable discovery these symphonies were for me. The Fifth and Seventh are particularly striking, while the Ninth is both profoundly odd and truly devastating. They deserve to be heard as much as anything by Tippett or Vaughan Williams. I've said my piece about Malcolm Arnold's neglect before, but what it has made me reflect on now is how terribly ephemeral critical consensus really is. Mahler, the blockbuster of the concert hall now, was never that successful in selling his symphonies to the concert programmer, while Bruckner was perpetually ridiculed as a simpleton. In fact, we can name and shame any art by mentioning prominent figures unjustly ignored in their time, artists forced to starve in their garret, novelists reduced to churning out monthly potboilers, film-makers desperately mortgaging their houses to finance completion of a soon-to-be award-winning masterwork.

But with classical music, I think until recently this allocation of merit had become quite settled and permanent. The greats were Bach, Beethoven, Mozart, Wagner and possibly Schubert. Beneath them was an honourable collection of fastest losers: Haydn, Brahms, Bruckner, Mahler and possibly Schumann. This was just how it was. Add to that a separate collection of twentieth-century giants (Stravinsky, Sibelius, Schoenberg and possibly Shostakovich), and that was it. The debate was over, the list finalised and nailed to the front door of every concert hall.

Now that seemingly permanent consensus is beginning to thaw. The recorded music revolution has allowed us to bypass the concert programmer and seek out works of outstanding merit that fall outside the accepted pantheon of the greats. Franz Schmidt's Fourth Symphony and Herbert Howells's *Hymnus paradisi* are my two suggestions for canonisation. I'm sure you will have different ones. But that's precisely my point; diversity and range, the impossibility of ever nailing down what makes great classical music, is surely essential to the survival of the form. Look at how controversial and often confusing is the debate over 'authentic' instruments; no one here says there's a right way and a wrong way to play Handel. Instead, we beg to differ over a variety of suggestions. But if we can't agree how to perform a composer's music, what right have we to judge on what rung of the critical ladder that music should be placed?

As the recording and distribution of music becomes even easier, this questioning of the critical consensus has accelerated. Look now through a typical edition of *Gramophone* and we see that advertising space goes more and more to recordings, not of the established 'greats' but of new discoveries and expansions of the repertoire. For every Simon Rattle and *The Planets* there's a CD of symphonies by Kurt Weill or piano sonatas by Dussek. For every Mozart, a Hummel; for every Shostakovich, a Vainberg.

Now that music can be downloaded straight from source, the opening up of the catalogue has accelerated. Where once there was a rigid canon, there's now the near-total anarchy of the availability of everything. That, of course, poses its own problems. Not all of this music can be great. While it's good we're being left more and more to decide for ourselves what makes great music, it's also clear we need help sifting through the mountains of obscurity. It's important we have voices pointing us in the right direction.

There'll always be a need for critics and commentators. Magazines like *Gramophone* depend on that need. But the electronic revolution has put critics in their place. A few healthy question marks have been attached to their role. They're there to offer advice, and not dictate. It's a humbling experience. But not unusual. Over the past few years there's been an explosion in blogs. These now number the hundreds of thousands. I think it says much that throughout this revolution no one has at any time suggested it would be a good idea for every one of these blogs to have its own review by a critic. That, in itself, seems a pretty definitive judgement.

fact. 'Avant-garde' sounds like an archaism from the 1960s. This should encourage us not to take these labels too seriously. As musical works once at the vanguard of modernism now start melting into the long, continuous stretch of the past, they seem less frightening, more part of a rich tradition. *The Rite of Spring* still has the power to excite and thrill us, but no longer produces the urge to riot. Debussy, so much an unusual sound at the time, now seems perfectly right. And as these individual revolutions fade slowly into the past, we can compare them more readily with pieces written one, two, three hundred years earlier. Ligeti's Requiem, for example, with its multiple vocal lines, produces a sonic chatter that can at times seem no different from parts of *Spem in alium*, Thomas Tallis's great forty-part motet written in the 1570s. Can four hundred years really separate these noises?

I suppose what I'm doing here is the aural equivalent of squinting: partially closing the ears so that two things which would otherwise seem perfectly distinguishable from each other become slightly blurred, revealing similarities in the underlying shape. It's quite a revelatory exercise. Another Ligeti piece, *Lontano*, when heard this way, seems not a million miles away from Sibelius's *Tapiola*. I have a recording of Glenn Gould playing Haydn piano sonatas that sounds in places like Oscar Peterson improvising jazz. One of the strangest pieces of Stravinsky I know (in fact, one of the strangest pieces of *music* I know) is his *Symphonies of Wind Instruments*. It's a mysterious succession of blocks of sound, self-contained little bursts of wind-writing punctuated by silences, building up over twelve minutes or so into something solid yet mysterious. Distinctly modern. But also not vastly different in shape and impact from one of Gabrieli's great wind sonatas and canzonas written for St Mark's,

Venice, more than three hundred years previously. Berg's Violin Concerto sounds modern, but has an emotional impact that turns technical fad into something timelessly heartfelt. The allusion to Bach's chorale in the final movement signals Berg's desire to affirm the long tradition he was now part of.

I suppose 'modern' becomes frightening only when we think it means 'frightening'. And that's most likely to happen when we approach a piece of contemporary music full of fears of what it might mean, of whether we'll have to cope with strange dissonances and a lack of identifiable melody. The sounds of classical music I was most drawn to on the radio were the mysterious ones: strange noises, arresting cacophonies. I loved the weirdness of Xenakis and Stockhausen and Charles Ives and many 'modern' composers whose names I didn't catch and who've now sunk into oblivion. Not only was I hearing noises I'd never heard before, they were so strange it was as if these composers knew these were noises no one had heard before. I'm still convinced that some children will be as bowled over by a blast of Ligeti as by the *1812 Overture*.

If we leave behind the easy categorisations – this piece is 'difficult', 'structurally complicated', etc. – and allow ourselves to respond to the music as we think fit, then we might be less bothered by whether we consider the piece modern or not. 'Modern' seems to me a label that can be attached to any piece written at any time in history that feels like it's breaking free into new territory. It's why, for me, Tallis's *Spem in alium* is as modern as Stravinsky's *Rite of Spring*.

By Special Arrangement

Much of our aesthetic experience is the product of a com-
mittee. Think of what the senses take in on an average walk
through the town: posters by the bus stop, the music in shops,
the design of a building, the look of a pair of shoes – all of it
is the end result of an awful lot of meetings. The Fiat Punto
is not the whim of an individual. At home, our experience
of the media and entertainment, even of pure art itself, is
affected by the input of many people: the newspaper editor
who decides a story is worth pursuing or a stitch-up worth
launching; the 'reality' show which is actually the product
of many hours' editing; the portrait by a famous painter, but
of a subject that's been chosen by the commissioner rather
than the artist. This column is, of course, written mostly
because I want to write it, but also because I'm contracted
to, and its shape and argument are subtly determined by
the number of words I'm restricted to (it will also have been
minutely pruned and anonymously improved by a helpful
sub-editor, who will already be nervous that my brief, to talk
about classical music, has not been adhered to throughout
the opening sentences).

In music, too, the autonomy of the composer and his or her composition is modified by practical, real circumstances. Poverty frequently forced the issue on accepting a commission, while a very realistic assessment of the local musical talents available would have determined instrumentation or the range of skills required to perform the piece well. The greatest composers, of course, produced works that burst beyond the limitations of the forces for which they were first composed. The converse of this, though, is that these compositions aren't necessarily the only true, immutable expression of the musical idea forming in his or her head when the piece was first written. Bruckner neurotically revised and revised earlier scores, and the fact that Bach, for example, could plunder previous cantatas and sonatas to refashion the material into later concertos and solo instrumental pieces, or rearrange pieces (not always by himself) for different instrumentations and treat these as new works, suggests we should maybe be a bit more relaxed about how we handle the originals. After all, before recordings existed the only way music lovers could really get to grips with new pieces in the home was through piano transcriptions.

A couple of recordings of familiar pieces in unfamiliar arrangements have come my way, throwing up interesting new reactions to how I now listen to the originals. The first is a recording of Bach's *Goldberg Variations* arranged for string trio (Julian Rachlin, Nobuko Imai and Mischa Maisky). The *Goldberg*, of course, has already gone through one instrumental transformation; purists still argue for the harpsichord, but most of us can happily live with the piece played on the piano. The move to string trio, however, seems less natural. It takes the Variations into a fresh sound world, a sound that's strangely like that from the late-eighteenth- and early-nineteenth-century salons of the affluent and cultivated, for which young Beethovens and Schuberts were supplying chamber pieces. The long, languid Variation 25 at times suggests even Schumann.

The piece sounds almost like these things, but not quite. The music of an earlier time can still be heard, but as if from this later perspective. It's unsettling. What it does, I think, is remind the listener that the time between the death of Bach and the advent of Beethoven and even Schumann was no greater than, say, the time between Schoenberg and Boulez, or between Britten's *Peter Grimes* and Thomas Adès's *The Tempest*. We spot continuity between these more recent musical events, but we put periods from the past into discrete, separately marked boxes. Re-playing them differently helps blow the dust off.

Similarly, I came across Mahler's *Das Lied von der Erde* (Ensemble Music Oblique/Philippe Herreweghe) rearranged for a small chamber orchestra by Schoenberg and Rainer Riehn, and hearing the familiar in an unfamiliar setting threw up new connections. I would never have compared Mahler with Stravinsky; but now, hearing Mahler pared down to the bare bones, the connection is obvious. The way both composers dot their themes around the orchestra, having the material bob from one instrument to another, never settling in one part of the orchestral stage, was, we forget, revolutionary when pushed by Mahler, acceptable and thrilling when developed by Stravinsky. The lushness of the larger Mahlerian orchestra perhaps drowns out the fact that barely a dozen years separates the composition of *Das Lied* (1907–9) with Stravinsky's *Symphonies of Wind Instruments* (1920). In chamber form, the connection is obvious.

In both cases, then, a fresh perspective encourages a closer look at the original. In skilled hands, rearrangement is revelation, not desecration.

A Sense of an Ending

There are pieces of music that remind me of certain paintings by Turner. It's a very specific similarity, so let me explain. The collection of Turners housed in Tate Britain in London gives a fascinating depiction of an artist discovering his voice. Any paperback edition of colour reproductions should do the same. From skilful but traditional countryside landscapes at the start of his career, in the late eighteenth and early nineteenth century, to rather more idiosyncratic, sometimes blazing, depictions of ships at sea, in the 1830s and '40s, all a whirl of colours, golden reds, large black clouds pouring out of the sky, the black almost taking on a life of its own and spilling down onto the sea, it's possible to read a story of a young artist gradually maturing, finding his own true voice.

But the real revelation comes at the end of the collection, the impact of which has stayed with me for more than thirty years. In Turner's last paintings the reds and golds and blacks have so taken over that the pictures look like nothing more than abstract discussions of colour. They have titles that imply they are depictions of reality (*Sunrise with a boat between headlands*, 1835, *Procession of boats with distant smoke*,

Venice, 1845) but what's on the canvas seems pure abstract art, not dissimilar to Rothko.

Coming to one of these last paintings in isolation, the viewer might think Turner mad. But I remember the real thrill came in working one's way towards these pictures and sensing how they seemed the inevitable conclusion to a process that had been steadily developing.

There are moments in music where this memory of Turner's last, amazing pictures comes back. These moments arrive, I think, when you follow the works of certain composers who, all the time they are developing their voice, seem committed to coming up with sounds that are idiosyncratic or aim to push traditional forms to breaking point in unexpected and sometimes wilfully eccentric ways (the Berlioz, for example, of the *Symphonie fantastique*, or Charles Ives in more or less everything he wrote), and then, at the end of their career, when they reach full maturity, produce work which defies categorisation, seems totally unlike anything else ever written, and yet which also feels like the inevitable consequence after all the work that had gone before. It's almost as if the composers come up with works that defy even their own expectations of what they can do.

Beethoven's last string quartets have always felt like this late Turner to me; works that are built on a lifetime of writing for those forces, and yet this time written through with a wilful disobedience of the standard rules of quartet composition, whether in length, number of movements, or in the development of the material. Sometimes amazingly sombre and controlled, sometimes defiantly playful and eccentric, everything preceding them seems just a learning process and what we're witnessing now are the fruits of that lifetime of development. In the late quartets I always hear the sound of Beethoven saying, 'At last, this is really what I've always wanted to say. And now, so confident am I in my ability and understanding of what music can do that I no longer fear the lack of convention I'm about to follow, nor the criticisms my contemporaries will no doubt heap upon them.'

It's an example of what I can only describe as heightened unusualness, as if the composer has stopped writing for anyone else other than himself (possibly not even himself), despite the oddness of what he's producing. These moments are everywhere. They're there in the strange dissonances of Mahler's last symphonies, especially in the shrieks surrounding the long trumpet notes in the Tenth Symphony. They're there, being rehearsed in Sibelius's Fourth Symphony, an exercise in the almost wilfully downbeat and morose. Neilsen's Sixth Symphony has it, too. This is a baffling, eccentric work, full of strange percussive ruminations and comic effects, sudden changes of gear and volume. It is, to put it bluntly, a weird work, as if defying anyone to work out what it's all about. And yet it seems to occur naturally after the adventures Nielsen conducts in his Fourth and Fifth Symphonies.

And these moments of heightened unusualness need not sound abstract or avant-garde. For me, the best, most sustained example is Bach's *Art of Fugue*, a set of works never attempted before or since, written for no public, given no specified instrumentation. *The Art of Fugue* is a law unto itself: a sustained example of heightened unusualness in music, seemingly written for no reason at all other than that it simply had to be written, as if all the work preceding it was a rehearsal for this purpose. Which is why I can find no way to respond to it other than by comparing it to the oddest of visual art.

Going Solo

Like an idiot, I only found out about the recent series of Daniel Barenboim recitals of all the Beethoven piano sonatas at London's Royal Festival Hall long after the entire set of concerts had sold out. However, I did catch an extremely thrilling performance of the last sonata, Op. 111, played by the young French pianist Cédric Tiberghien one lunchtime at London's Wigmore Hall and the memory of a packed hall frozen in utter stillness as the second of the sonata's two movements drew to its serene close reminded me of what a supremely odd thing it is to be in a large hall listening to just one performer.

These performers give their all to the performance, and seem so intensely preoccupied with each note they're probably unaware of anyone else in the room. The whole spectacle seems intimate and yet, being a spectacle, and a popular one at that, it demands a large space from which the thousands can view the intimacy.

There is something inherently odd, I think, about hearing music performed on a solo instrument for any sustained period of time. We feel we shouldn't be there. Surely this is

the player's moment, and not the spectator's. If it's a recording, we feel that perhaps we can't give it the sort of focused
attention it deserves. Solo instrumental music, for example,
is not the sort of thing one would put on in the background.
Its versatility and virtuosity, the sheer chutzpah in making
an instrument momentarily sound more than the sum of its
notes, demands total acknowledgement and respect. That's
why I find these pieces when they're at their best utterly fascinating. They tread an intrepid line. The precariousness of
what they're trying to pull off makes it all the more satisfying
if they achieve it. The best pieces for solo instrument rely on
disorientation. This is music at once celebrating the range
and subtle timbres of the instrument – a sort of manifesto
of what the instrument can do – and yet simultaneously an
attempt to break free from that instrument's limitations,
momentarily to delude the listener into forgetting he or she
is hearing just one sound. You hear a Bach solo cello suite
and you are impressed by the emotional as well as technical
range of the cello, while forgetting it's just one cello in the
first place; the music builds to a complete picture every bit
as detailed as something provided by a quartet or a small
chamber orchestra. I'm aware I keep coming back to Bach but
I have to mention now that all the drama, emotional journey
and technical subversion displayed in the long Chaconne at
the end of Bach's Second Partita for solo violin makes it, for
me, the summation of solo instrumental writing; it creates a
world that seems, for the duration of the piece, much larger
than anyone could reasonably think that instrument was
entitled to.

There are other more recent masterpieces of solo music.
The second half of the twentieth century seems to have
thrown up some fine examples, of which Britten's marvellous

Cello Suites, written for Rostropovich in the 1960s and early '70s, spring automatically to mind. I've lapped up Luciano Berio's mad, ambitious, almost unstoppable series of *Sequenzas*.

To return to Barenboim, pianists are at an advantage in that the keyboard is probably the one type of instrument that we would naturally expect to hold its own as a solo medium. Indeed, it's so self-sufficient that it's always seemed unnatural to see a piano sitting in the middle of a symphony orchestra. But even here there's a disorientation. Piano music, as with any solo instrument, takes us a little bit more towards the performer and away from the composer. The great musical index resonates with the name of great pianists such as Horowitz, Richter or Gould, whose playing personality seems so much part of the music they're performing. This writes large what I've always felt about listening to solo instrumental music; that we step a little bit away from the composer, and indeed the time in which the piece was written. Maybe it's because the musical palette has been simplified, but I always find it difficult, or it takes me a little while longer, to put a composer's name to a piece of solo music that I'm hearing for the first time. And even then I'm usually wrong. It's another dislocation. One can inter-mix the piano music of, say, Bach and Shostakovich, without too much of a glitch, in a way that one really can't with their orchestral music.

But I like this. Listening to the solo instrument takes us slightly out of time, away from biography, and into the sudden focus of music examining its own limits.

Beyond a Joke

Very often, it's the interpretation of the weakest or least appealing moment in a piece of music that can determine the quality of a performance. I often decide how good a Beethoven symphony cycle is by how well they play Symphony No. 6, the *Pastoral*. This is because, out of all the Beethoven symphonies, the *Pastoral* is the only one I find tedious. I tend to skip past it, finding it languid, static and, apart from the storm, unengaging. I hear myself sighing if a radio announcer tells me with great pleasure that the second half of a live relay is going to be taken up with it. I go and watch the news. So I like Nikolaus Harnoncourt's Beethoven cycle best of all, because Harnoncourt's *Pastoral* is brisk and lean, and diverting all the way through. He makes me want to listen to it again. The other symphonies are even better, of course: it's a fabulous set of recordings, and straddles an amazing balance between the techniques of original instrumentation and a modern orchestra (the Chamber Orchestra of Europe). The performances are consistently fresh, delivering for the listener that experience which all great interpretations bring: a sense of what it must have felt like to encounter the piece for the very first time.

I'm sure we all have little blank moments where, no matter what the critics tell us or what the audience numbers demonstrate, we simply don't buy into something that so many others clearly enjoy. For some people, it could be a composer (a London orchestra is currently marketing their Brahms season with a poster campaign shouting 'Brahms: You Either Love Him or Hate Him'). For others, it's a single work that they just can't get to grips with: usually Messiaen's *Turangalîla-Symphonie*.

For me, it's a symphonic movement. You see, for all my love of orchestral music, for my delight in the symphony, I continually have problems with one movement in the classical symphonic structure: the scherzo. Beethoven invented it, and did wonders with it. But it's a joke. A light-hearted piece of merry-making which, in the *Eroica*, Beethoven took to a demonic level. But why, two hundred years on, do we still see the need for it? Opening movements are grand statements of intent. Finales can provide drama and satisfying resolution. Adagios create stasis and beauty, a pause for breath between two areas of intense activity. But why the scherzo, other than to show what the orchestra can do when its back is against the wall and maybe it's got an expensive guest conductor who wants to make a splash? The scherzo frets and twiddles and can, on occasion, seem a rather puncturing parody of what's gone before.

I enjoy Bruckner, but find his scherzos mind-numbing. They feel like he's writing them against his will. The other movements, the drama, the reflection, the titanic struggles, he can do well: they come from the soul. The joke, the larking about: that doesn't come naturally to Bruckner, and consequently his scherzos can sound forced and rather laboured, like a serious man being asked to come up with a funny. The best Bruckner conductors, therefore, will be the ones who can make those scherzos sound fresh. Bernard Haitink does it for me.

Two of my favourite symphonies from the twentieth century have two of the most original scherzos. They're the Symphony No. 1 by Walton, and Shostakovich's Tenth. Both their scherzos come second, as if to insist there's no let-up in the drama, and both are relatively short in comparison to the rest of the works in which they sit; about five or six minutes long. Shostakovich is violent and full of bluster. But, this time, the bluster doesn't seem like a parody. Shostakovich can frequently pad out his symphonies with ironic re-creations of state-sponsored spectacle, pompous marches and screeching bands. In this scherzo, there is no veil of imitation; this is the real thing, huge brass beats looming nearer and nearer like an army about to trample over you, and a savage rhythm that consistently threatens violence. For a scherzo, this is no joke.

While Shostakovich frightens, Walton menaces. His short, sharp scherzo is written to be played *con malizia* (with malice) and in the best hands it can be a deeply unsettling five minutes. Waltonesque syncopations suggest something jolly, only to be suddenly spat back at you at twice the speed from the brass. There's a constant drive forward and back, a pulse that keeps tapping forward then doubling back on itself, like a lion looking round for somewhere to lunge.

After both these short, sharp shocks from Walton and Shostakovich, their respective slow movements come as welcome pauses for breath. Hearing it all again, I'm reminded of what a good scherzo can do. It's not a little game to be played in isolation of the rest of the symphony; the best symphonies are those where the scherzos have become fundamental pieces of the drama.

Living with Mahler

Gustav Mahler was born in Scotland in 1975. His first work, the mighty Sixth Symphony, was premiered there around this time, in a bedroom on Glasgow's Byres Road. It was played on headphones, since the venue was also shared with an older brother who liked Pink Floyd.

The performance was a great success and led to a rapid outpouring of other symphonies from Mahler. In chronological order these were the Fifth, Second and Tenth, leading to his most recent work – the Seventh. All of them have received full performances on loudspeakers, and one or two of them in the concert hall.

In the early 1980s, Gustav Mahler went on to produce his great song cycle, *Das Lied von der Erde*, and later some of his earlier pieces. He's still alive, but hasn't written anything for twenty years; his last work being a discarded movement from the First Symphony, premiered in 1989.

I'm sorry if that brief biography of Mahler didn't quite tally with the facts as you know them. But then, what facts do we need to know when listening to music? The facts as I've written them form a crude portrait of my experience of Mahler's music, and for me are a perfectly valid starting point when trying to describe a character or personality in the music that I've lived with for most of my life.

There is, I think, something special about the relationship we have with a composer's music. It becomes a living, evolving thing, and it's remarkably different from the bond we form with, say, a literary work, or film, or piece of sculpture.

Music is the replication of a sound first produced twenty or even two hundred years ago, yet it can't be pinned down through touch or sight or description. It's a living thing in the room, stimulating immediate emotions that can't be reproduced by other media. Music is pervasive, yet evasive.

We live with music in a way we can't live with a book or a painting. Explosive streaming content now allows us to watch any film or TV show repeatedly if we want to, but how many of us actually do? Yet we can live with Berlioz's *Symphonie fantastique* all our lives. That's what I find fascinating about exploring a composer's music: that it can grow into a consistent psychological presence; a sort of invisible friend, who stays with us through trauma, house move, marriage, illness, education, school runs, sackings, debt, or loss. We steadily know the music, so that it becomes for us a background personality, as familiar and human to us as a cousin or aunt.

For me, to live with Mahler's music means building an impression of a voice or personality in that music, different from the historical figure who wrote it and separate from any technical analysis of the composition. I often thought the same way about writing – about whether we read, say, a novel or even a newspaper column with our own constructed 'voice of the author' in our head. This would usually bear no relation to the physical voice of the writer. I think it's a pity that columnists' photos now appear above their commentary in newspapers or online. It somehow spoils the purity of the voice and personality we've constructed from the writing to see a gawping bald man and unfashionable shirt at the top of the piece. We're encouraged all the more to create a voice from music, simply because we're dealing with a sound. It's as if the music colludes with us in improvising a fictional personality of the composer, different from whoever actually existed. Knowing the historical facts behind a work may help clarify or focus the listening experience, but they don't always help. For example, I'd far rather enjoy Wagner without having to contend with the fact he was a pompous racist.

Mahler's was the first music I grew to love, and the affection hasn't diminished. Along the road, of course, I've become besotted with and inspired by other composers – by Bach and Shostakovich and Britten especially, and more recently Stravinsky – and there have been one or two periods of a year or more when I might not have listened to any Mahler at all. But that didn't weaken the bond. Like with any good friend, the connection remains just as strong. The conversation is picked up from where it was left off, after any long absence.

So why do I form my connection with Mahler? It may be because Mahler's music was one of the first I came to listen to, and for a very mundane reason. I joined the local library, which had a well-stocked classical music section, but being under fourteen, I couldn't take more than two recorded items out. Looking for quantity rather than quality, I was intrigued by Mahler's symphonies, most of which were so long they spilled into two discs yet still counted as one item. I quickly did the maths: two Mahler symphonies were four records. I'd legitimately beaten the system! The perfect crime.

When I got home and listened, again and again, to his music, I was instantly puzzled and intrigued. It was wonderful, but sometimes dreary. Vulgar at times, but also rapturous. Sometimes repetitive, but more often than not exciting. Dramatic, emotional; occasionally excessively so. If I were to explain retrospectively why his music had such a pull, it may have been because of this messiness, the sprawling untidiness and unevenness of the symphonies. I liked that. It made him seem more human, less inclined to conform to a system or authoritative template of how orchestral music should be written.

I'm someone who has never seen the point in having to make decisions, and who would, in a perfect world, prefer to defer all decisions to the day of judgement. So maybe I rather liked the fact that Mahler thought the symphony should be all-embracing and universal. That it should touch on song, and childhood, and death and nature, and consist of programmatic as well as abstract argument. It is, of course, an excuse to justify lack of focus and too many movements, but I still find it endearing.

Perhaps, in my middle age, I can see, for example, the opening of Mahler's Ninth Symphony as a tentative lyrical farewell of a troubled man, poised at the edge of modernism, living with a fatal illness, yearning to push his romanticism to the limits of what the new century could bear. But do I need to apply this experience to the innocent ear? After all, I can't shake off the mental image I formed when I first heard this beautiful swaying rhythm thirty-five years ago: that of a small ship, loaded and leaving the shoreline to cross an expansive sea, perhaps never to return.

Why should I rationalise my identification with Mahler's music after the event? At the time of first listening, when I

didn't know what I know now of Mahler's radical new meth-
ods of orchestration, flitting fragments of themes and motifs
around the orchestra from instrument to instrument so that
no single instrument takes the lead, or secures the theme for
itself, but instead using the orchestra as a whole; as one giant
instrument played with force or subtlety as the composer
sees fit. Not knowing all this, I still felt I'd stumbled across
sounds that I knew were the ones I'd most want to hear again
and again. The great choral climaxes of the Resurrection
and Eighth Symphonies, the delicacy of the songs, the hymn
music which closes the Third, and the brave silence which
finishes off the Ninth. Or that extraordinarily distant confrontation with chaos that he was mapping out towards the
end of the Tenth Symphony, when he died.

What was Mahler doing? What was he up to? It was
the questions his music asked, rather than any answers
it provided, that made it so fascinating and which makes
speculation about what he may have produced had he lived
longer an absorbing game.

And following Mahler's music, watching the evolution of
his style across nine symphonies and an uncompleted tenth,
is a thrilling journey. The First opens with a strange, glowing
hum of harmony. The Tenth's most memorable moment is
a huge, shrill wail of discord from the whole orchestra, an
enormous shriek of pain, ugly and atonal, like a scar across
the world. What comes in between is an adventure.

Remarkably, with each symphony Mahler writes in a
style that is always identifiably his own, and yet also creates
a whole new sound world unique to that symphony. The
Second is grand and defiant, the Fourth childlike and sparse.
The Fifth is a celebration, the Sixth tragic and intense. The
Seventh is mysterious, defying categorisation, an hour of

unsettling 'night music'. The Eighth is a great wall of sound, the Symphony of a Thousand, with many choirs, choruses and soloists daring to portray a vision of heavenly love. The Ninth is wide-ranging in emotion but rigorously written, beautifully structured and with a shattering ending in which, for the final three minutes, Mahler comes as close as anyone to composing a musical representation of silence.

His death was truly tragic because it ended an artistic career so clearly on the verge of a major innovative phase.

But in saying all this, I'm aware that I can sound as if I'm defending Mahler, pushing for him to be considered top musical dog. He wasn't the greatest composer who ever lived; I probably reserve that title for Bach or Beethoven, though you might have other suggestions. I know Mahler – though great – isn't the best, but that's not the point. Neither was he perfect as a man, and that too is irrelevant. I'm talking instead about a bond we form with a certain composer's works. Whether it's an emotional or intellectual one, it's essentially human and it remains strong despite the flaws and imperfections we discover along the way.

I, for example, have always had trouble with Mahler's middle movements. They're never quite as serious as his outer movements. They seem a little mundane. Little points being stretched to eternity. For maybe a decade or more, I'd even come to skipping through them when listening on CD. Now I'm more patient; I enjoy the delicacy, the eccentricity. But listening to them still feels faintly like work, though work I'm happy to undertake. Mahler's character, too, feels rather unsettling: a tyrannical conductor, a man happy to abandon the Jewish faith of his birth to gain promotion in a Catholic society. An angry, emotional neurotic. Do I really want to know him?

I hold another personality in my head: that of the body of work, the voice of the music that survives the discovery of such flaws. The only image I can come up with to get anywhere near illustrating what I mean is if you think of the example of a true friend. A true friend is someone who knows you intimately enough to recognise your faults, and yet who's quite happy to stay a friend. The knowledge of failings is something that, on paper, should prove divisive, but in fact seems to strengthen the bond. If you were truly friends with someone, you would visit them in prison even knowing they'd committed a crime. Many have been recently flocking to see the final works of Caravaggio. Extraordinary works of art produced by a man on the run for committing murder.

A composer's music is never free from the context of the composer's life. But if my hunch is correct, to many of us it somehow seems autonomous. So, for example, while we may think it valid to strive to perform the music as close to how the composer intended, the music itself has a much more vibrant life distinct from the conditions of performance. More importantly, it means that many more of us should feel free to participate in discussions about the music we love, without feeling we have to have the full biographical facts or technical knowledge at our fingertips. And yet our enthusiasms, somehow, are kept private. There's no musical equivalent of the book club. I think this is sad, as it leaves us all communing with no one, apart from with the partly fictionalised but always alive musical personality that we love listening to.

Gustav Mahler was born on 7 July 1860. Poignantly, he died only fifty-one years later. Those are the facts. What feels to me true also is that his death brought to a sudden end a startling cycle of great symphonic works that journeyed from brilliant, ostentatious orchestral impressions of nature and folksong, through lengthy studies of emotional turmoil and finally, under the strain of the heart condition he knew was going to end his life while still in middle age, in extraordinary last symphonies exploring the darker and more extreme reaches of what orchestral music can achieve.

Finding Schumann

Can a moment change everything? On hearing one little passage of music – nothing grand, a short phrase, a bar even – can one's preconceptions about a composer's music be completely overturned? I think so. It's recently happened to me. I'd always regarded the music of Robert Schumann a no-go area. Now it's becoming an obsession. In the past, when trawling through CD stalls, I'd quickly leaf through all the Schumann and move on to the Stravinskies and Shostakoviches and Schmidts and Schnittkes, stuff that seemed much more immediately meaty and relevant. Schumann I'd always imagined as too refined and precious, a drawing-room ornament displayed as one would an antique vase, to be approved of rather than enjoyed.

Someone once described his music to me as 'fragile' and I automatically assumed he was using this word pejoratively. It's interesting how one grows up with assumptions and unchallenged judgements. Certainly, as I came to classical music, I came also to an image of what classical music it was that I wanted to hear. Boldness, noise, sweep, range, ambition. Immersed in surround-sound composers like Mahler,

Shostakovich and Wagner, I was suspicious of anything that smacked of timidity. Romanticism had to be whole-hearted and full-blown or it wasn't true to itself; looking back, I can understand why someone in his teens or twenties would believe this, but now it seems at best a barely acceptable naivety. Back then, there seemed nothing to be learned from what sounded to me the music of the privileged, sheltered salon; trios and quintets and Lieder that seemed, to my over-opinionated ears, to be the background noise of a complacent, comfortable environment, chamber music composed and played in a small part of Europe, commissioned by the rich and performed in the homes of the imperious and untroubled.

Of course, Schumann's life story is not that of an untroubled man; hounded by a bully for daring to love his daughter, married to a talent that seemed publicly to overshadow his own, and eventually victim of an illness that robbed him of his sanity. But that was not something I ever let myself hear in the music. Instead, this life's work seemed to be something of a no-man's land, a gap between the more interesting spaces occupied by the revolutionary energy of Beethoven and the charismatic romanticism of Berlioz and then Wagner.

Then I listened to *Dichterliebe*, sung by tenor Werner Güra, with Jan Schultsz on piano. And there are three moments which changed everything. The first comes at the end of the tenth song, 'Hör ich das Liedchen klingen' ('When I hear the little song'): the love-sick poet hears a song that reminds him of a girl who's spurned his advances, and his 'overwhelming pain / Finds relief in tears'. At that point, the singing stops, the words are over, but the piano carries on, as if to another verse, but one that never comes. The notes trickle down like tears, but there are no words. It's a fine dramatic moment, poignant, even painful; this is no song cycle for salon friends.

Bach in Space

When I first heard some of Bach's Solo Violin Sonatas and Partitas, I instantly thought of outer space. Maybe I happily made the association because I grew up with moon landings and Kubrick and have always been a little obsessed with what on Earth (or, more accurately, out of Earth) is going on in the vast darkness of the universe. There was something about the purity of the sound, the one violin somehow becoming a whole world, that made me think of a small voice making contact, breathing life, out on a large and unending stage.

I wasn't the first, of course, to link music with the heavens. Kubrick seized Strauss and Ligeti for his *Space Odyssey*, Patrick Moore grabbed Sibelius for *The Sky at Night*, and any *Horizon* documentary on deep space or interplanetary travel will usually feature a complex computer simulation of a pilgrim spaceship gliding across screen to some slow, majestic music from Wagner or Bruckner.

But these are all the whims of programme-makers. What I found particularly gratifying to find out was that NASA scientists actually agreed with me on Bach and the violin. The two Voyager satellites, which left the Earth's orbit over forty years ago and are now the first man-made objects to leave our solar system, have on board a set of golden discs containing sights and sounds of Earth. These discs are designed to show any inquisitive aliens who may stumble across or whoosh into them that we're a peaceful, talented and fundamentally tuneful lot. One of these sounds is Arthur Gumiaux playing the Gavotte en Rondeaux from Bach's Solo Violin Partita No. 3. The disc attempts a comprehensive survey of man's music, and includes everything from Azerbaijani bagpipes to Chuck Berry's 'Johnny B. Goode'. Mozart, Beethoven and Stravinsky are represented, but it's interesting that while others get one mention, Bach is the only representative of humanity whom NASA scientists felt deserved now fewer than three tracks to himself. The Voyagers also house Glenn Gould playing a Prelude and Fugue from Book 2 of *The Well-Tempered Clavier*, and Karl Richter conducting a *Brandenburg Concerto* (the first movement of No. 2).

Why Bach? Is it because his music sounds so elemental? Is it because it concerns itself with structures and patterns, fugues and the recurring circles of the formal dance, that it feels less like the personality of an individual and more the basic, representative language of a type of thought; as if Bach came up with a series of musical building blocks that have formed the foundations of the modern Western classical music tradition? I've read this theory often enough; the argument that somehow in his counterpoint and inversions and double- and triple-fugal patterns Bach has set out the musical equivalent of a mathematical system, and unnervingly tapped into a pretty fundamental code that lies at the heart of how we think creatively and aesthetically.

It's a pretty grand claim, but not one I'm entirely

comfortable with. First off, it all but ignores the sheer quality of Bach's music, concentrating instead on shapes and structures. It's the life Bach breathes into otherwise cold calculus that sets him apart. And who could listen to the formal technique on show in the extended Chaconne in the Second Partita and not hear something passionate there too?

Bach was the first to explore certain music forms, but also the last. No one has bettered the six Cello Suites or the solo violin music; Shostakovich only managed one Book of twenty-four Preludes and Fugues, not two, and nothing comes quite so close to the oddness of *The Art of Fugue*. Is there anything in the canon of Western art that can match the *St Matthew Passion*? Bach can't be diluted into a symbol of universality because he remains so stubbornly individual. Maybe it's the humanity, then, that NASA felt drawn towards.

The human touch brings me to another fanciful notion I've had about space and music. All the images we have of the Universe are images of the past. We see a galaxy through a telescope, but the light from that galaxy has taken millions of years to get to us. We're looking straight into time gone. It's history, but it seems to be living in front of us. Similarly, when I listen to music, especially to early music, before Bach, right back to the early work of Léonin and Pérotin at Notre-Dame Cathedral in the twelfth century, laying down systems of rhythm and notation that were the foundations of how we write and play music now (available on a Naxos CD), I get this same sense of being lucky enough to hear the past as if it's still happening. Maybe because music is a sound, something intangible and yet present, it occupies this strange space between the past and now, between reproduction and reality, and that makes it so curiously in here and yet out there at the same time.

Unheard Of

The recent commemoration of the 150th anniversary of Elgar's birth may incidentally have reinforced a few misconceptions about British orchestral music. So great is the First Symphony, for example, that it's easy to accept the conventional history that it came out of the blue, that Elgar had no recent, collective British-based symphonic tradition to draw from, that he was left alone to come up with the first English musical masterpieces since Purcell.

In fact, as recent Stanford, Parry and Bantock discs show, there *was* a British symphonic tradition; Elgar's achievement was that in one fell swoop he wrote something that went straight to the top of the pile.

Enterprising releases from labels such as Lyrita, Naxos and Dutton confirm that Elgar was also not a one-off, and that he re-energised an extremely creative half-century of sometimes outstanding symphonic cycles from British composers. Malcolm Arnold wrote nine, many of them quite electrifying. Edmund Rubbra produced eleven, of great craftsmanship and lyricism; indeed, the opening to his Fourth is one of the most beautiful openings of any symphony written in the twentieth century.

Literally hundreds of British symphonies were written in the first two-thirds of the twentieth century. Sturdy old Havergal Brian wrote thirty-two, the last eight of which he produced in his nineties. Just issued are forgotten symphonies by Richard Arnell, Gordon Jacob, Edgar Bainton and Rutland Boughton. Why have I never even heard these names before now?

It would be wrong to expect all the symphonies to be masterpieces, but neither should they be dismissed as trivial. The opening of Arnell's Third, for example, is unforgettably thrilling and expansive. This is not the 'cowpat' music people so often think was all Britain produced before Birtwistle and Maxwell Davies.

Indeed, here's another preconception about twentieth-century British orchestral music that simply doesn't stand up to examination: that all of it was the mushy, pastoral outpouring of a group of folksy traditionalists. Again, the misconception is linked to a popular figure whose work has to fight against a fixed but inaccurate interpretation: our most popular symphonist, Vaughan Williams. Because the first three of his nine symphonies are concerned with extremely English notions of the sea, London and the countryside, the rest of his music has become lazily described as pastoral or even parochial. The violence of the Fourth Symphony and the rigour of the Fifth and Sixth should have put paid to that, but an image, once fixed, seems very difficult to dislodge. And so we have lumped together the likes of Vaughan Williams, Holst, Howells, Butterworth and Finzi into some collective syrupy movement of riskless conservatism that the new British musical establishment in the 1950s and '60s declared was harmful. Far from it. Robert Simpson's eleven symphonies sound more modern European than British, Humphrey Searle's eight symphonies travel towards atonality, while Arnell's rarely settle into anything comfortable and quiet. Alan Rawsthorne's three symphonies are all tonal but troubling. His second is called *Pastoral* but it's very much a countryside of cold winds and harsh winters. These works remind me of a phrase William Walton used to describe the brutal, fast short second movement in his First Symphony: *con malizia*, 'with malice'. Malice runs through the twentieth-century British symphony with surprising regularity. Whether collectively these composers were railing against the neglect they were experiencing, or whether their music can't help but be touched by the upheaval of two world conflicts, I can't determine; but what seems crystal clear is how fundamentally serious and certain they are about what they want to do. The British symphony is unsettling, not comfortable.

If nothing else, I urge you to listen again to what I think is the most unjustly neglected of symphonic cycles, that of William Alwyn. Alwyn wrote a lot of powerful and famous film music and perhaps his success here contributed to the neglect of his more serious output. But I find his five symphonies punchy, violent, tuneful, succinct, wonderfully orchestrated pieces packed with ideas and energy. Malice and brilliance are found in equal measure. They deserve to be played as much as anything by Tippett or Walton. And yet they're not.

And neither are any of the symphonies I've singled out. One thing Britain has led the world in musically has been our huge number of neglected composers. It's a curious denial of a crucial component of our national heritage. This is how a country responded musically to important times and yet awkward attempts have been made to silence it. Fortunately, readily available downloads and moderately priced CDs are now putting things right and allowing the listener to decide whether this legacy deserves to last.

How Good is Mozart?

And so to Mozart. He really can't be put off any longer. I've spent so much of this book talking about the composers I've liked or have grown to like and about how I'm constantly amazed, overpowered even, by classical music's extraordinary range and diversity of styles. To those who criticise this music for its supposed elitism, old-fashioned stuffiness or downright exclusivity, I've tried to give examples of where it can surprise, challenge, experiment, use tradition to comment on the contemporary and, above all, communicate in a way no other medium can.

Which is why I've resisted bringing Mozart into the argument for so long. You see, my approach as a listener to his music has always contradicted the open-mindedness I've urged in others. For too long I've had a bad attitude to Mozart. I've been turned off by his popularity. I've used his sometimes saccharine, childlike melodies to dismiss his entire catalogue as nothing more than ingenious variants on 'Twinkle Twinkle, Little Star'. I've never been able to sit through a production of *The Magic Flute* without thinking it's probably the silliest, messiest story I've ever seen. I've gone off in a huff and put some Wagner on instead.

Now, of course, I've kept this quiet. It wouldn't do to say publicly that you just didn't 'get' Mozart. The man's held in such extravagantly high esteem (I remember a BBC Radio 3 interval talk about thirty years or so back in with Bernard Levin, crusading around the festivals of Salzburg and Vienna, started praying, actually praying, to Mozart as the one piece of humanity that was the embodiment of perfection and immortality) that maybe it appealed to the mischievous side of my nature to lash out against this collective brainwash.

Interestingly enough, whenever I've summoned the courage to admit that Mozart simply passed me by, leaving me unmoved, I've been surprised by the number of people who agreed. They confessed it furtively, looking round just in case any cultural stormtroopers were gathering on the other side of the wall. It was like belonging to some dangerous secret club; not one that met every week to plan insurrection, but which did quietly wonder aloud whether Haydn might actually have been better.

And yet, and yet. I can't put Mozart fully out of my mind. There are some pieces of his, residual moments, that have made such a profound and lasting impression I simply can't get rid of them. The overture to *The Marriage of Figaro*, for example, seems to me quite the happiest piece of music written. The final movement of the *Jupiter* Symphony feels like the most overwhelming tumbling-out of ideas and energy compressed into an unbelievable ten minutes. Once, suffering from terrible insomnia as a student, turning the radio on I heard the beautiful, achingly simple tune starting the slow movement of the Piano Concerto No. 27 and it suddenly made absolutely every stressful component of my circumstances seem utterly stupid and unnecessary. If this music was childlike or innocent, it was innocence reimagined by a mature mind.

Now, as I stumble awkwardly through Mozart's music, I realise that what I've railed against is not so much Mozart as the image the world has presented to me of Mozart, the gifted, prodigious, ostentatious child who never grew up and who churned out effortless chocolate-box melodies and preferred relentless beauty and harmony to anything troubling or revolutionary. Once I leave this contrived fiction behind, I start encountering great music: the best of it catches my attention precisely because it seems most un-Mozartian in its style. There's a jaw-droppingly original *Adagio* movement in the Serenade for Thirteen Wind Instruments, a daringly sustained heartbeat throughout, over which solo lines play off against each other and all seem so delicate and yet rooted in this persistent pulse that doesn't let up. It seems brave rather than sweet. I'm surprised by the amazing originality, and then control, in the *Dissonance* Quartet; I've got a recording played by the Belcea Quartet on EMI and they don't play it like 'Mozart' but like this was a late Beethoven or a mighty Brahms. In short, they play it like it's a masterpiece, which, for me, it suddenly is.

This is the start of a long journey. I'm still put off by the little nursery-rhyme tunes, but these, I notice, are all in the early works. What's dawning on me is that the real Mozart, the Mozart I'm getting to marvel at, the Mozart of originality and experimentation, when his heart as well as his ability matures, starts flowering in the last four or five years of his life. It makes the Requiem all the sadder since it marks the end of an artistic life that was clearly on the verge of something even more profound.

The truth is only just dawning on me: Mozart is going to be the most difficult composer I've come across, because it's going to take me a lifetime to work out what I make of him.

Rameau's on his Own

I'm sitting on my own in a characterless hotel room, next to a plate of individually wrapped shortbread biscuits and a plug-in hairdryer, and all I've got to listen to is an overture by Rameau. It's the overture to *Les Indes galantes*. It's enough.

Until recently, I'd never knowingly listened to Rameau. His is one of those names I've heard often, like Lully, Couperin, Schütz, even Liszt, who've seemed unread books to me. These names are great blanks in my musical knowledge, taunting me as much as I'm taunted by not having read anything by Henry James, Anthony Burgess or Samuel Richardson, or by not knowing much about the paintings of Poussin or the films of Jean Vigo. These names remind me that all I'll ever know in a lifetime of trying won't be enough, that certain people have sweated a life of creativity I'll simply never get round to doing anything about. There's simply too much stuff to know, I tell myself, so why can't I be left to enjoy the works I got to love early on in life without feeling pressurised into sampling everything else there is?

And now I've got fourteen hours or so, in a pinkish room with powerful air conditioning and no soul to speak of, and all I've got with me is a single piece of Rameau. But that's fine.

Though I've never carried in my head an idea of what essence of Rameau sounds like, in the way I can with, say, Bach or Stravinsky, his name usually suggested to me the word Baroque, and that word always seemed to carry with it a rather pat, confined musical impression. Baroque music is, I thought, light, and clean, and sharp, and brisk. A starter rather than a main course. Nothing too serious or substantial. But above all, I thought, it's music of another era. It's historic, in the way that much Romantic music, because it's so overtly emotional, appears not to be. But the Rameau I'm listening to now, in this rather characterless room with too many pillows and not enough blankets, has a gallop and liveliness that instantly dismiss these deaf preconceptions.

For a reason I now can't quite remember, I recently wiped most of the music on my phone. I think it was displacement activity instead of writing. Time to refresh my mobile listening. Chuck out all the Haydn and Shostakovich, make way for some Walton or Nielsen. But I chose not to delete this piece by Rameau. The music intrigued me. It's from an album of his overtures, played by *Les Talens Lyriques*, conducted by Christophe Rousset. I bought it second-hand, on a whim. Rameau, I thought, Baroque music: music to work to. Pleasant. But it sounded so fresh I stopped working and started listening. It seemed so well thought out. Here was a voice, not just a name from an old era or a bit of style. And in the overture to *Les Indes galantes*, an opera by Rameau about which I know nothing, but which I now very much want to track down and hear, there crept in a jaunty, rather jazzy theme – the only word I can think of to describe it is a jiggle – one which seemed so contemporary and unfussy and which playfully pushed the rest of the piece along in such a sparky and surprising way that I instantly heard a living personality behind the music. The notion of a distant age suddenly seemed nonsense.

I never got round to putting the Nielsen and Walton into my phone, so here I am in a depressing bed-in-a-box next to some glossy lifestyle magazines and a TV that has Sky Sports and a channel devoted to hotel information, with just a single piece of Rameau to listen to. And that's fine. It strikes me, hearing the Rameau, how patronising we are about progress and the passing of time. We assume that what comes later in history must be so much more sophisticated than what came before. So, in music, we can't but help feel that the full modern symphony orchestra is much more complex and sensitive a beast than anything an earlier age gave us. We assume that, to put it bluntly, we're better than they were because we know so much more about what music can do. That's why I – and I'm sure many others – have fallen into the trap of thinking Baroque and early music are somehow less subtle and interesting than the music that followed.

For me, hearing that selection of seventeen overtures by Rameau, each of them sounding fresh and original, even contemporary, makes me realise that in its clear lines and brilliant phrasing, Baroque music has an intelligence and integrity that I've previously missed. Suddenly that era doesn't sound so far away at all. And it's a deal more interesting to listen to than the noise of the air conditioning.

Four Movements

I: Allegro, ma non troppo

I often think Haydn gets a raw deal for writing 104 symphonies. Choose any half-dozen at random and they'd easily be considered a fine body of work from a fine symphonist (I'd make a special plea for No. 22, *The Philosopher*: a beautiful and original statement of the form). But 104 of them! Try as hard as you can, no one will believe you if you argue they all merit repeated playing. There are just too many, people say. We can't help but look at Haydn as the Barbara Cartland of symphonists. It's as if fecundity was the opposite of creativity.

No, nine has become the conventional badge of excellence. I can't help thinking we subconsciously judge a composer's merits as a symphonist by how near he gets to writing nine of them. That puts Schubert just below Beethoven, but higher than Schumann, which seems about right. So, Sibelius is marginally better than Nielsen – seven to Neilsen's six. And so on.

It's a stupid game, but I do wonder if we'd treat Haydn's symphonies with more respect if we just batched them in bunches of nine and regarded each batch as the product of a different master. So 104 divided by nine makes Haydn 11.55 great composers. That sounds about right.

II: Adagio

Mahler was famously haunted by the fatalistic notion of writing a ninth symphony, and dutifully died before completing his tenth. Mahler was the first composer I became obsessed with (no doubt following the lead of a good many other adolescents) and an obsession with the form of the symphony has stayed with me since. It's perhaps why I grew up thinking the symphony had to be a major statement, an important creative drama, a universal sweep of emotions. For me, classical music *was* the symphony. Starting my musical life with Mahler made it more difficult to take seriously any composer who failed to produce a symphony. It was almost as if the likes of Debussy and Ravel hadn't got any clout. Now, of course, I know differently, but it makes me sad that composers don't write as many symphonies today as they used to.

III: Scherzo

In 1907, on a visit to Finland, Mahler met Sibelius, and the two of them clashed over what a symphony was about. Mahler stated it should be 'like the world. It must be all-embracing' in response to Sibelius feeling it should instead have a 'severity of form' and a 'profound inner logic'. You could argue that the same contrasts were being played out a century earlier between Haydn and Beethoven. Although Haydn's symphonies got longer towards the end, they always remained tightly constructed, and seldom lasted beyond twenty-five minutes. Beethoven took the symphony and turned it into both a personal manifesto and a statement of the universal. The *Eroica* was revolutionary not only in length but in its declaration of what music could do. Music as an abstract drama or narrative. Music no longer as a background rhythm to a masked ball, or the soundtrack to worship. Music is given its own new form. Farewell to the minuet and hello to the scherzo. Music is divorced from function and placed centre-stage. And we surround it. The *Eroica* honoured the act of listening. We no longer had to be doing something to hear good music. Instead, we were asked to perform a more demanding activity: to sit down and do nothing but open our ears.

IV: Finale

I was wrong to measure a composer's virility by how many symphonies he wrote. Where would be Bach? Emasculated. But I wonder why we don't hear so many new symphonies today. Is it just economics? Is it too much of a financial gamble to programme thirty or forty minutes of new music played by large forces? If so, then it's a cruel irony that the form that honoured the active listener is now considered too demanding a listen to put in front of him or her.

Or is it that the symphony is considered old hat, as out of date as a Victorian novel or bone china tea service – great to preserve, but too ridiculous to copy? Then maybe, since much contemporary music seems to be revisiting the purity and simplicity of form of early music, paring down players, simplifying structures, avoiding the grandiloquent state-ment, just maybe a new composer can go past whatever excesses they see in Mahler, past the egoism of Beethoven,

The Shadow of Death

How abstract is music? Not vocal or ceremonial music, but pure instrumental, chamber or orchestral pieces, written as if in entirely abstract forms: the symphony, the quartet, the sonata. How easy is it to come to these things with no preconceptions, no prior knowledge of the biographical circumstances in which they were written?

Shostakovich's centenary year has thrown this issue into sharp focus. Much has been written about how necessary it is to listen to the man's music with a definite awareness of the cruel emotional stresses Stalinism had imposed on him as he was writing. To listen, we're told, we first of all have to know ... know what conditions Shostakovich was living under, know what his state of mind might have been at the time, know why he was writing the way he did. Subtle arguments have raged over how much we need to see the likes of the lengthy bombast of the Seventh Symphony's opening movement as 'ironic'. So that what some people detect as flaws in the composition are, others insist, dramatic, even deliberately melodramatic, exaggerations trying to communicate something of the hysteria surrounding anyone trying to be creative in Soviet Russia in the middle of the twentieth century.

I can't help feel, though, that the pressure is on us to make Shostakovich one of the exceptions; that the critical climate is for us to value purely abstract music as superior in form to anything which carries an explicit narrative, or an implicit dependence on outside knowledge of biographical or historic facts. So, the tone poem is regarded as inferior to the symphony, for example. This is understandable. What we so often recognise as precious in music is that whatever special magic or meaning it conveys is communicated in a mode which is beyond language, nationality, or, even, personality.

And then I heard Shostakovich's Viola Sonata and everything turned on its head again. The sonata, the final slow movement in particular, is one of the most beautiful, anguished and intimate pieces of twentieth-century chamber music I've heard. Gone is the bluster of the symphonies. There's a pain here that's not dramatic but real. But it is also the last piece he wrote. How much does that matter? Does it make any different listening to it without this knowledge?

My instinctive reaction is to turn that question on itself: what does it do to the music knowing it's the last thing Shostakovich wrote? Knowing that he knew he was dying. Though it's possibly to treat pieces such as the Viola Sonata as purely abstract musical forms, and to get an enormous amount of pleasure from them, knowing something about the circumstances in which they were written offers an additional pleasure. It's not an essential knowledge; the piece doesn't fall apart without it. But it adds something indefinable, a resonance, as we listen.

It struck me as I listened that perhaps the whole debate about Shostakovich and the political circumstances he lived in is a red herring. There's a far more significant context we perhaps subconsciously call up and apply to music, and that is a knowledge of where it comes in the composer's life. You can't doubt, for example, that the popularity of the *Pathétique* Symphony, Strauss's *Four Last Songs* or Mozart's Requiem owe an awful lot to our knowledge that they came at the end of each composer's life. The disintegration of tonality in Mahler's Ninth Symphony and the incomplete Tenth is particularly the logical next phase in the progress of his symphonic cycle, but must also have been influenced by the knowledge he was dying.

One can easily slip into a morbid school of thought, turning the works into freakish curios rather than treasures because of their association with death. None of them would have survived if it was not a blazing work in its own right. But I would like to place a question mark against the notion that the more abstract a piece of music is, the more perfect it becomes. I'm always struck, listening to a Mahler symphony, by how much I automatically hear connections or references to the symphonies that come before it and am alert to new sounds that anticipate passages from ones that come after. I can't help but listen with a memory of the other works he wrote.

I'm sure this is all a fundamental part of the listening experience. Who can claim, for example, to listen to Beethoven without being impressed, forced even, to connect the music to the personality of the man? And anyone who stuck with Radio 3's Bach Christmas marathon, where every work of Bach's was played over a ten-day period, will testify to how much their appreciation of each piece was enhanced by the fresh memory of the other works that surrounded it.

The magic of music is bound to its fragility. Music lives

Silence and Sibelius

It's often fun to hear how the critics got it wrong, praising Salieri over Mozart, dismissing Bruckner as a simple
provincial, laughing at Mahler's ridiculousness, rioting at
Stravinsky, possibly admiring Bach's dexterity at the keyboard but side-lining his compositional talents as the work
of a man pig-headedly stuck in the past.

I was reminded of this while reading a *New Yorker* article
by Alex Ross on Sibelius's missing, long-awaited, never-
heard and probably destroyed Eighth Symphony. Ross paints
a picture of a composer who may have achieved popular
international acclaim, but against whom there was a vehe-
ment critical backlash. Consider, for example, the influential
critic and theorist Theodor Adorno's claim that 'the work of
Sibelius is not only incredibly overrated, but it fundamentally
lacks any good qualities'.

These words astonish me. Sibelius, perhaps more than
any other composer, has been my gateway to classical music.
The ruggedness, beauty, thickness, tenseness of the noise
that I heard when I first listened to the opening of the Third
Symphony settled it for me: classical music wasn't the fey,

light-headed, drippy background noise for 'cultured' people to play at dinner parties; it was so much more, something quite powerful, deeply human, the most natural music in the world anyone would want to make.

The more I heard of Sibelius's music, the more inspired I was to explore. His symphonies led me on to Neilsen, Shostakovich, Britten, who in turn brought me to Janáček, Prokofiev, Rachmaninov, Tippett and Walton, who then introduced me to Grieg, Tchaikovsky, Bartók, Elgar, Bax. And so it goes on, pushing forward, delving further back. The concentration of form in Sibelius's Seventh Symphony even brings you to Webern.

Since all musical impressions are terribly subjective, I'm not sure it's worth even attempting to reach a definitive conclusion regarding right and wrong in the critical battle over Sibelius's music; far better, I think, to pause and reflect on what all this tells us about the inconsistencies and contradictions we apply daily to music.

Yes, we want to hear stirring originality, we want our expectations confounded, the comfortable status quo shattered, and yet we also flock to hear the reassurances of acknowledged masterworks or rediscovered treasures. Anything too difficult can prove troublesome, yet anything too familiar can appear light. The tension between our yearning for reassurance and our appetite for surprise probably runs through our response to the last hundred years of classical music far more substantially than we might think.

For while it's possible to trace a coherent line of development through, say, *The Rite of Spring* and Schoenberg and the Second Viennese School, on through Boulez, Ligeti, Xenakis, Cage, Berio, Birtwistle and Stockhausen – modern adventurers prepared to face audience opprobrium and initial critical confusion in return for expanding the limits of musical expression and performance – it's also possible to draw a parallel, more lyrical line from Mahler, through Strauss, Sibelius, Neilsen, Shostakovich, Britten, and on to, say, MacMillan and Adams today. Their work gains its strength from how well it connects with its audience, using complexity and even perplexity as a finishing point rather than as a starting position.

This second group seems more interested in the musical journey, while the first concentrates on presenting the listener with a new and untested musical world right into which he or she has to plunge immediately, with all the trauma and exhilaration that can bring. Both seem to me equally important.

Similarly, it's possible to come up with a workable division of composers: those who originate, innovate and develop fresh forms, and those who follow, take existing forms, but push them to their highest mark of quality. One could place Beethoven, Bach, Haydn, Wagner, Stravinsky, Schoenberg in the first camp, and, say, Tchaikovsky, Mozart, Bruckner or Schubert in the second. Shostakovich strengthened the symphony and quartet rather than revolutionised them, so Camp 2. Bartók, however, mounted a more radical overhaul of the orchestra and quartet, so Camp 1. Again, no one's professing one camp to be better than the other, and the enterprise has something of a parlour-game feel to it. But it does, I hope, reinforce the importance both traditions in twentieth-century music have for our understanding of the art today.

Respect for tradition can be just as potent as a radical desire to revolutionise. After all, Bach, that arch-conservative,

A Life at the Opera

Opera is the coming together of music, theatre, design, people and coughing in the greatest synthesis of art capable of collapsing at the beep of a watch alarm. It is man's highest creation, his most expansive assertion of artistic supremacy over the inferior beasts and birds of nature who, proficient though they might be with sticks and spittle, can't perform tricks as staggeringly complex as mounting a three-act declaration of love from a wooden castle. Foxes don't sing and leverets are incapable of costume design, so they needn't bother trying. Armies of termites, though they may impress us with their twenty-foot-high mud constructions, haven't a hope in hell of building anything out of wet dirt as architecturally elaborate as a publicly funded opera house, with its dazzling honeycomb of boxes and its awesome web of sturdy crush bars. Have I made myself clear, animals? We're better than you, so go back to doing what you do best, which is sniffing at bushes.

This is what opera is. It's the rustle of programmes and clack of glasses cases of several thousand people anticipating grandeur. A few are celebrating their birthday, many are romantically involved with others in the audience, some are dying, several are currently being burgled, one or two are planning to run away tomorrow, five have grit in their eye, one lost her dog to a temporarily out-of-control recovery vehicle that morning, more than you think are currently passing on an unpleasant dietary virus to their neighbour, over a third will find the evening didn't quite match their expectations.

The conductor. Was knighted five years ago for making terrifying demands on his horn section. Is a single man, dedicated to music and bitterness, secretly nurturing a reputation for shambolic jacket/trouser coordination so it may procure for him that title of 'genius' which the newspapers have so far forgotten to award. Has the pervasive breath of claggy mint gums, which he regularly puffs across the violins and cellos, who call him Menthol Mickey in tea-bar rehearsal breaks.

He comes on.

The audience now applaud the respect and admiration the orchestra fling at him in his pit. From this underground nerve centre, he bobs his little white ground-levelled head round to smile at the line of eager and disappointingly shod feet he's playing to in the front-row stalls. As the applause dies, he catches sight of a slightly furled sticking plaster jammed under old tights, badly masking a moon-shaped scab on a thick leg, and turns to start the music.

Music. Strange, this, coming from under the stage, and for the first ten minutes all we've got to look at is a heavy curtain with the crest of a crowned unicorn mounting a heron. But the first notes strike us as lovely and we start giving the experience the benefit of the doubt. Meanwhile, the burglars jemmy their way in through an upstairs window and start looking for the plasma telly. The rustling in the circle falls to a minimal patter as the music swells. People do hold their breath like they're meant to; though one individual is just frozen in the sudden realisation she forgot to book a clown for tomorrow morning.

The Prelude to *Tristan and Isolde*. It lays before us the themes which will dominate the evening's performance. Wagner's peculiar chord near the start, pinpointing everything from Isolde's doomed love for Tristan to Tristan's extraordinary annoyance at having his emotions jerked around by somebody's love soup, crowded onto a little blurt of sound that the programme notes tell us turned the music industry upside down. For years after the first performance, people went around whistling the Tristan Chord, which they would normally have to do in groups of seven, or on their own if they happened to have a uniquely damaged mouth.

The music continues, and Menthol Mickey's arms form spindly shadows on the front curtain, attaching giant black rotating antlers to the head of the raped heron. This is passionate music now, and the sound from the orchestra slushes and glides around in a slowly blossoming wallow. The audience make last-minute assessments of near neighbours, calculating from the frequency of coughs and the guessed texture of the liquid mix jumbling around inside whether the offenders are having a final clear-out or are digging themselves in for an evening's phlegmish sabotage. This uncertainty threads uneasiness through a few minds, one of which now fills with pleasing images of the gentleman two rows in front having his mouth stifled with a trumpet and a hammer.

The music reaches a peak of intensity symbolising Tristan and Isolde being at it like knives, and three rows from the back, inside a small woman, on her upper gums, four from the left, a tooth begins to hurt. The tooth was attended to yesterday, didn't like the experience and has now decided to give his owner a little nudging reminder of what he can do when he puts his mind to it. 'I dutifully masticate for you, my lady governess,' he professes, 'and I yield to your brushing and scraping without qualm or worry. I sit guard for you all night, and I endure deposits of nut and tomato skins with openness and true hospitality for these, my new visitors. And, lo, you reward me with drills, and my payment is needles. My heart is hollowed out, and filling composite occupies my soul. Is this, then, how my service is spurned, oh wicked lady? Am I an outcast on your gums? Then I shall make known to you the vent of my fury, by summoning the twang of my brother Root and sister Nerve. Feel you now the power of my anger? This is naught to the suffering I can assemble if you shame me with full purpose!' His owner makes a mental note to book a further appointment.

The music diminishes, and the curtain rises as the thieves find the plasma screen and start disconnecting from the wall. In a house four miles away, a professional clown who had been expecting a call that day sets off disappointedly for a walk in the night, realising the tomorrow morning which he'd provisionally set aside for work will now be wasted. This is the fourth disappointment in as many weeks, and propels his mind closer to thoughts of retirement. The curtain carries on up to reveal the drift of the evening. The arrangement of shapes and colours on stage will determine whether an audience smiles at the welcome arrival of an old friend, or frowns in anticipation of an evening blighted by modernism, like a dinner spoiled by a daughter's art-school boyfriend.

This evening falls somewhere in between. Familiar bits of building and rampart are hung in a peculiar combination (one man is upside down) but the settings are shatteringly far from the Cornwall of the original story (Act One takes place in a European sauna). It's apparent the audience will have to do some work for their average of ninety-four pounds.

And over there are the soloists, Isolde bound against her will for a forced marriage with an enemy despot while harbouring unrequited love for her father's killer, and her trusty maid telling her it could be worse. As they sing and towel themselves in the shadows and beautifully lit darknesses of a guarded steam room, it's clear this evening we're going to be in the company of an Isolde who is colossal.

Opera can be unkind to the massive. It thrives almost exclusively on prolonged demonstrations of love and captivating beauty, yet has constructed traditions of vocal power and range that demand these love anthems be projected from a big chest. Bulky singers have to fight against the obvious stupidity of the undertaking by producing sounds that transcend girth, and hoping to God the director doesn't ask them to roll around in an upstage forest glade. This is the governing doctrine of our highest art.

Later, we find that Tristan too is colossal, so the love story does at least carry some conviction. Whether that's enough to conquer the mounting ludicrousness of the artistic proposition offered this evening will take at least another four hours to determine. Despite some knowledge of the music, despite even a familiarity with the peculiar habits of opera, there is still a detectable, sniffable gas of suspicion wafting across the audience that they have paid to watch a huge bad thing. Apart from the disgusting size of the participants, a hundred other points of absurdity produce dangerous sparks.

That faint creak and wobble of the scenery; the thickening grills of sweat down Isolde's back whenever she sings near the charcoal briquettes; the sometime written randomness of the melody; the moment when Isolde's maid snagged her scarf on a small handle jutting from a boat at the back of the stage made from fridges; those points of loudness and loftiness of pitch that unavoidably turn in to a pained shrill (two thousand knees are briefly tensed); that unfortunate play of light and shadow which at one point projects on to the backcloth a silhouette of Tristan, short and stumpy, save for a pitilessly elasticated stomach. The evening could go up in flames at any moment.

And yet the music just about banishes that threat. Out of passages only moderately captivating come regular bursts of overwhelming glory that grab concentration, dim pulsing teeth, usher someone away from thoughts of baking, another from planning tomorrow's elopement, a third from still-felt contempt for his doctor. As the sounds soar and mingle perfectly, the evening makes sense, the stupidity is forgotten and the burglars and the rain and the hundred cars outside and the fight forty yards across the street and the disgruntled clown and this morning's news about the Egyptian president and the pictures of his collapsed bike are now nowhere, and then someone sneezes, which is when, somewhere in the middle of Act Two, in a radical switch to the American Midwest, we return to a stage full of big people and papier-mâché cacti.

The evening tos-and-fros between these two states of appreciation. The music constructs an opera of ideal beauty and total tragic conviction, while our eyes apprehend something tiptoeing on the borderline with the abysmal. These two forms happily gallop in parallel, but occasionally merge in magic moments of believability, when for a brief second the only thing that seems real is an enormous couple singing German laments about fatality while wearing Stetsons and rejoicing in love at a Kansas rodeo. Once the magic is dissipated, by the drop of a purse, or the demented half-time rush of the parched to the interval bar, like bison to a breeding ground, leaving Tristan, now kebabbed on someone's spear, to die in German out of every one's hearing, slowly fading while tethered to a still-moving mechanical bucking bronco, it's once again easy to gaze at watches and flick through programmes, and to take in wider views not only of the stage but of the conductor's feverishly bouncing head demanding adoration from a bassoonist being slowly suffocated in a cloud of stale peppermint, and wider still to see the patchwork of cemented haircuts along the front rows and gaze up to the sides of the building, noticing the boxes from which people view events from a severe angle, and to wonder what the Queen makes of all the performances she is forced to see bent round at seventy-nine degrees, and whether she remembers the evening not for what she saw on stage but who she was staring at across the theatre. What must life be like when viewed constantly from a right angle? Did the Queen grow up thinking that all playwrights stage dramatic action to take place out of the corner of one eye? Does she have her favourite sides of actors? Does she consider Shakespeare to be our greatest slanty dramatist? Has her right ear grown to twice the size of the left? Funny things, ears. Two gnarled flaps of flesh hanging from the face, like skin from an old pair of cheeks retrieved from the waste-paper basket for alternative use. Starched face-flannels. The only parts of the body to look like Ireland. Which is better than looking like Egypt, which surprisingly is almost completely square. All that

War Weary

As we continue our endless War-on-Terror-and-Isis-and-Insurgents-and-Saudi-Funded-Jihadists-and-as-inevitably-as-night-follows-day-now-Trump's-in-charge-Iran-and-North-Korea, there will no doubt soon be a whole catalogue of musical works that celebrate, commemorate or commiserate the frightful mess we seem to have made of the world. At stupefyingly awful times like these, the composer becomes political, emerges as someone who feels obliged to come up with a definitive response to international events.

John Foulds' *A World Requiem* was one such piece, written not long after the First World War, celebrated after its premiere at the Royal Albert Hall in 1923, hailed as an immortal masterpiece not long after, then forgotten. It was recently rediscovered and performed, and the release of a recording on Chandos seems a useful opportunity to ask if there's something that typifies music's approach to war; not to its martial celebration, but in response to the aftermath, the dawning reality that destruction and death inevitably bring rare rewards. In particular, the revival of Foulds' work makes noted British musical responses to war such as

Michael Tippett's *A Child of Our Time* and Benjamin Britten's *War Requiem* seem less like highly idiosyncratic personal responses to global catastrophe and more part of a living tradition.

In Britten's *War Requiem* the religious backdrop is dramatic and ritualised, on the verge of being satirised, even. Britten's 'Dies irae' is almost a commentary on Verdi's. The standard sections of the Requiem Mass are performed by enormous, loud, sometimes shrieking forces. This is only a remote picture of heaven, and a very immediate vision of hell. Some critics have found the Mass elements rather forced; as if Britten is going through the gestures of composing a Mass for large numbers when what he's more interested in doing is presenting the more intimate and moving works of Wilfred Owen. Personally, I find they work brilliantly, but only once you regard them as dramatic devices. Seeing the piece performed live clarifies the purpose: the massed ranks of chorus and orchestra are pushed back, with some choirs expressly positioned in the distance. At the front, in a more intimate configuration, are a small chamber orchestra and three soloists. The effect is simple, but unforgettable; voices of the individual, singing poetry of intimacy and pity, against a backdrop of ritual.

If in the *War Requiem* the religious backdrop is kept deliberately artificial, in *A Child of Our Time* it is when the most overtly religious texts push through, in the form of traditional spirituals, that the humanity is most strongly asserted. The spirituals are musical statements of fellowship and of survival. Against the bleak narrative of Nazi persecution, they offer a release into something resembling light. Again, this is music written to have dramatic impact. It's no coincidence that *A Child of Our Time* is structured in three parts like *Messiah*. Britten and Tippett are writing to the British tradition of public oratorio performance. The children's choirs, the hymns, the chorales; these are part of a long, amateur performing culture: local choral societies who spend a year rehearsing *Elijah* or *Gerontius* for one big charity concert, or local orchestras who mount *Messiah* in a day.

Foulds' *A World Requiem* provides a more explicit link between the later works and the tradition from which they spring. Written not long after the First World War, it is a work praising the faiths and peoples of all nations. There are powerful and moving passages that hint at what Tippett and Britten were later to achieve, but on first listen *A World Requiem* reminded me mostly of Elgar and in particular *Gerontius* and *The Apostles*. Foulds' work provides the perfect bridge between the nineteenth- and early-twentieth-century choral society culture and the more political and emotionally charged war works by Tippett and Britten. In its appeal to 'the Chinaman and the Muslim' it's very much of its imperial time, but also summons moments of anger and musical originality that transcend this. A deeply experimental, questioning work lurks within. This should come as no surprise. The English oratorio is a melting pot of other traditions. England's most popular composers were Handel and Mendelssohn, who weren't even British, and Elgar, whose unabashed Roman Catholicism has never stopped *Gerontius* becoming a concert favourite.

Foulds, Britten and Tippett were idiosyncratic, independent artists. They write about a war that tries to crush human spirit. Through their work, individuality becomes a symbol of universal humanity. For these composers, turning personal feelings into public and popular statements becomes an act of creative obligation.

The Special One

Which composers matter? By this I don't mean who are the greatest, or which composers set the most successful trends. What I'm really getting at is, if very particular cyber-terrorists hacked into the digital database of every classical music publisher in the world and deleted their back catalogues, which composer would you miss the most?

I'm assuming there's no single answer. We'll all have our favourites. But I'll also bet that for most people it will not be an obvious choice. For someone's Bach, there'll be another's Busoni, for every Wagner, a Vaughan Williams or a Victoria. We form emotional bonds with music that often have nothing to do with the composer's historical impact. Sometimes a fond memory provides an association that, once formed, can never be weakened. More frequently, I think, we stumble upon a voice, a particular, identifiable, idiosyncratic sound that can belong only to a particular composer, and it's that sound that we warm to, no matter what the piece. I've started listening to Martinů, his Fifth Symphony, and I rather liked the noise of it. So I've gone on to hunt out more Martinů. To the extent that I can now recognise the Martinů sound whenever I hear it. I like it. I've no idea whether it's considered any good or not. I've no idea either whether I'm listening to late or early Martinů. I just warm to the Martinů-iness of it.

But when does this subjective fondness start to matter? Really, really matter? There are clear examples of it mattering for certain conductors or performers who've dedicated a large portion of their career to championing the work of composers who otherwise might not be considered for the canon of musical greats. Look at how Charles Mackerras has pushed and cajoled us into accepting Janáček, not just as an interesting twentieth-century Czech composer but as one of the greatest opera composers of the past two hundred years. Yehudi Menuhin's support and programming of Bartók was also significant, as was Colin Davis's obsession with Berlioz. People of sound judgement are saying, look, there's more to musical greatness than Bach, Schubert or Mozart, and more to musical impact than the revolutions of Stravinsky, Beethoven or Schoenberg.

Why they feel they have to put so much effort into promoting this music is perhaps because there's a tendency for us to try to categorise music, to place it within a style or a period; anything that doesn't seem to fit, any sounds that seems so idiosyncratic, as if it's come from nowhere and is possibly going nowhere, can sometimes get put to one side. We hear Berlioz, we may or may not like the Berlioz-ness of the sound, but we don't stop to consider whether this is music that really matters. Colin Davis has spent a career saying that it does.

What composers like Berlioz, Janáček and Bartók have in common is an air of having absolutely nothing in common with those around them. Berlioz's *Symphonie fantastique* comes only a decade or so after Beethoven, but is from another sound world altogether. In its orchestration, structure and

narrative it's a work that almost contemptuously defies categorisation. And the sound that Berlioz went on to make for
the rest of his artistic life, taking on mounting debts to do
so, bold, passionate blasts of brass and skittering strings,
was one of almost deliberate idiosyncrasy. I've always felt
this way about Janáček, too. Janáček's voice was always an
extremely eccentric one. It's difficult to compare his music
with anything outside itself. He absorbed folk rhythms, but
only into a musical language that was already distinctively
personal. He made the apparently straightforward seem odd.
I heard his *Capriccio* recently. A conventional name for an
odd combination of instruments: brass, flute and left-handed
piano. Listening to it, it's impossible to determine whether
this music is progressive or traditional, mainstream or avant-
garde. It slithers from one category to another because in the
end it is just Janáček. And we measure his music and how
good it is by that criterion alone.

More so with Bartók. His six string quartets make him
one of the most important figures of twentieth-century
music, but how often do we forget to include him in the
list of the 'significant'? How often is he left off the list that
includes Stravinsky, Schoenberg, Berg, Ligeti? Is it because
he attempts no conformity, he doesn't take on targets or aim
for categorisation? Even if it means he has to endure poverty,
exile, ill-health and neglect, he just sticks to the only thing he
can do: writing Bartók.

Our musical tradition is upheld and strengthened by a
long line of composers who sought nothing more than to be
themselves, and we can judge them only by how well they
did so.

Now's the Right Time
for John Adams

What are you like in a fight? I'm a bit of a wimp. I'm hampered by continually seeing my opponent's point of view. If someone came at me in a great rush of violence I'd both duck for cover and try to work out what I'd done that had made my attacker's actions objectively the only possible course open to him. In any controversy my default position is always, 'Well, what's wrong with both sides meeting somewhere in the middle?' That's why I'd fail as a politician. Attacked by my opponents, I'd probably think they've got a point.

In musical controversies too I remain stubbornly, immovably and unapologetically as wishy-washy as possible. In the middle of any argument over where classical music should be going, my impulse is to remain firmly perched on the fence. So, in the great fight between modernists and traditionalists my instinct is to think music too important to be confined to one school of thought. To the two feuding camps who declare respectively that music should either be populist and inclusive or dangerous and fearless, I again can't help but see the merits of both cases. That's why I think John Adams might be the most important composer writing today.

I say 'important' rather than 'original', or 'profound', or 'challenging' – though he can be all these things – because I think his music's greatest merit is that it draws in as wide an audience as possible to contemporary classical music and yet, without alienating them, can take that audience into provocative and unorthodox territory. His output is popular, his concerts are sold out, his music has commercial impact, and yet he never panders to the popular appetite. His operas, *Nixon in China*, *The Death of Klinghoffer* and *Doctor Atomic*, are all about near-contemporary international politics, bringing complex and otherwise off-putting subject matter to a mass and appreciative audience. These works have, in a single sweep, demonstrated how relevant opera as an art form can be today.

Adams's flight in the 1960s from New York to San Francisco is seen by many as a symbolic fleeing from the abstruse experimentation of the likes of Milton Babbitt and the atonalists who populated East Coast America at the time. The West Coast becomes, in this myth, a place where a composer is no longer embarrassed to work with melody, harmony and conventional orchestral forces in front of appreciative audiences. I think this myth does a great disservice to the challenging originality of Adams's music. *Shaker Loops*, for example, sets itself an extremely complex task: to keep a piece of music moving forward almost solely through the use of constantly driving yet subtly shifting rhythms. It's an experiment in propulsion. The miracle is that Adams comes up not with an arid exercise, but something which is startling and captivating to hear.

What Adams does in his best music is treat the listener

with respect. He produces work that makes listening a thrill. I can think of many great moments in Adams's music that made me feel when I first heard them that classical music was the most exciting, vital and satisfying form of music we've ever produced. And they still make me feel that way when I hear them now. One is the opening to the final section of *Harmonium*, settings for orchestra and chorus of poems by John Donne and Emily Dickinson. The final section, 'Wild Nights', starts off with a distant rumble in the orchestra that gradually and magically seems to get nearer and more complex, near-to-bursting with pent-up energy. As the dam of noise bursts, in comes the first chorus entry with an emotional cry, shout almost, of what seems like pure ecstasy. It's an absolutely spellbinding moment; a great unashamed affirmation of what contemporary choral writing can do.

I get a similar sense of pure excitement towards the end of the first section of *El Niño*, Adams's oratorio-like retelling of the Nativity story. The section ends with a marvellous Latin American poem describing a little girl trying to catch a falling star. As she catches it, she burns, and disappears in a glow of flame. Pain and ecstasy in the poem, the pain and ecstasy of childbirth in the Nativity tale, is matched by the most beautiful and passionate energy in the music; strings scuttle and scamper in a frenzy, the soloists rush, the chorus rhapsodises, and soon all the forces come together with the orchestra in an amazing glow that sustains longer than you could believe possible.

It's a tremendous, memorable, heart-stopping moment, and John Adams is capable of these on a regular basis. He is, for me, the composer working today who seems to write with the greatest sense both of the times he's living in and of the audience who need music to speak of these times.

Keeping it Simple

I've become obsessed recently with the middle movement of a Haydn Piano Trio (in E, H. XV No. 28). It's a slow, five-minute movement, starting with a tense, almost creepy stumble on all three instruments; but a few bars in, this suddenly gives way to a long, beautiful solo on the piano that expands for several minutes. The keyboard melody seems to come from nowhere, not even from Haydn. It certainly doesn't sound eighteenth-century: more like a piece of Bach that's been jazzed up by Jacques Loussier to make it more contemporary. The nearest equivalent I can think of is 'Air on the G String', but this is much more brooding and subtle. The two string instruments slide quietly, unnoticeably into background accompaniment as this long piece from nowhere stretches out into full form. And then, again without warning, the serenity is shattered starkly into a passionate cry from the whole trio, the melody quickened and jabbing, until, just as suddenly, everything collapses into silence. It's a profound and entirely original piece of music, and it provokes three questions:

1: Why isn't this piece more well-known? Why is it not trotted out in compilations of Calm Classics and Moody

Movements? Is it just a bit too weird or too troubled for that kind of thing? I think to myself of the unjust way we label Haydn a joyful and prodigious tunesmith, as someone who cheers us when we're low, but whom we seldom credit with profundity. And so he falls between two critical stools: too sophisticated to be commemorated on compilations of light classics, and yet too playful to be taken seriously enough.

2: Why didn't I know about this piece earlier? I assess my own ignorance. It's huge. But I've got used to that and, in fact, find it a source of consolation in an odd sort of way. When you think how many sub-categories there are of popular music, from be-bop to house to rap to punk to ska to rhythm'n'blues to torch song and on and on, with an ever-expanding list of sub-categorisations issued practically every month, and when you consider also how such a wide set of genres has fanned out over such a short period of time, over just about sixty years, is it any wonder that a listener to classical music can never reach a total and comprehensive understanding of all the music that comes under that label? That's about nine hundred years' worth of music! And most of our pop comes from just America and the UK. Western classical music comes from Paris, Vienna, Prague, Berlin, Venice, Rome, Budapest, St Petersburg and about a hundred other cultural centres of excellence that have risen and fallen over the course of a near-millennium.

It's no surprise, then, that most of us probably harbour secret worries that our knowledge of classical music is incomplete; and I've often thought the subject would be instantly more appealing to the novice if the bulk of us admitted the areas of our ignorance up front. I've come pretty late to opera, I know very little of German Lieder, and there are certain 'great' composers I'm still almost totally unfamiliar with, such as Chopin, Liszt and Dvořák. Yet, as I've got older, becoming aware of the near-infinite nature of classical music has brought me some consolation: it's so impossibly vast a source of material that only a superhuman freak can possibly feel knowledgeable about all of it. What's more comforting: to know that no music will now surprise you, or to realise that unknown gems are still waiting to be discovered?

3: Why have I come to it now? Or, to put is simply, are chamber works music for the middle-aged listener? As I get older, am I less impressed by the dazzle of the orchestra and more beguiled by the intimacy of chamber pieces? It's an easy argument to sink into. The young composer sets out to make his mark on the public with something spectacular, and the young listener is captivated by the result. An older listener likes to get the bare bones of what makes music work, how it moves and structures itself, heard in the starker context of a work for a few instruments. There's no science here, just speculation on my part.

But I wonder too whether chamber music is now the music of our time. That if classical music is going through a phase, just as pop music enters three- or four-year bursts of evolution every now and then, whether that phase at the moment is for the intimate chamber piece. Is there something in the marketing of young string quartet players posed in trendy clothes and moody lighting that acknowledges we have a growing appetite for the simple, pared down, unostentatious, deeply felt, intimately constructed composition? As religious devotion dies and information overloads, is it not then the case that we find ourselves drawn to music, like the Haydn trio that obsesses me now, that seems to speak directly and with an emotional honesty that we seldom find anywhere else?

Taverner v Tavener

In music there are of course two John 'Taverners'. The famous one (with the slightly different spelling of Tavener) – who sells CDs and downloads by the hundreds of thousands, wrote works commissioned by current royalty and whose *Song for Athene* became almost the defining musical moment at the funeral of Diana, Princess of Wales – was born in Wembley in 1944 and died in Dorset in 2013.

The other one, forgotten by many, one of the key composers of his generation, lived from 1490 to 1545 and wrote a stunning set of Masses for the new Anglican Church in turbulent Reformation times. A recent release of his *Missa Gloria tibi Trinitas* from the Choir of Christ Church Cathedral, Oxford, under Stephen Darlington, reaffirms what a glorious and innovative composer he was. The 'in nomine' section of the 'Benedictus' spawned many imitators and influenced a generation after him.

It's tempting to see these two composers as radically different in outlook and style. The popularity of the contemporary Tavener is frequently used by furious critics to indicate a lack of substance or complexity, the reward for a tendency to go for overt, repeated, palpable emotion rather than difficult, hard truths. Meanwhile, the earlier Taverner's fall into part obscurity is neatly hoisted as a badge of honour, a mark of the composer's profundity and depth of serious- ness. Here is someone, it's suggested, who may be neglected now but had integrity then, holding firm to the directness of his religious expression but never shirking from the structural complexity and innovation his music pushed him towards.

I've never felt that argument washed. Tavener, I think, rather bravely turned his back on what is presumed to be the classical music consensus. He intentionally wrote outside the modern Western European tradition and was drawn towards the language of the eastern Orthodox Church, which can at times sound alien and slightly baffling. His *Ikon of Light* (1983) for choir and string trio has great shrieks of joy from the choir, massive chords of a kind not usually heard in a cathedral, as well as moments of unsettling discord that suggest the chaos out of which harmony later emerges. It can be an uncomfortable listen.

I've also found his *Eternity's Sunrise* – a setting of words by William Blake for soprano, Baroque orchestra and hand- bell – a deeply moving yet innovative work, which sustains ten or so minutes of high-pitched, delicate sounds in a brave edifice successfully suggesting a childlike but honestly felt imagining of eternity. Mysterious and unusual, it deserves recognition.

But the rot set in when Tavener's large-scale work for cello and orchestra, *The Protecting Veil*, became a huge hit and topped Classic FM's charts. We don't like our classical music to be too popular, or gobbled up too eagerly by the rabble. I remember, when compiling a programme of my favourite music for a Radio 3 show, the looks of disquiet when I suggested some Tavener. Clearly, championing his music was not the done thing. Why not? Maybe those in charge of the canons of contemporary taste are uncomfortable with obvious religious devotion. Devotion to a god rather than to one's art maybe leads to a diminishing of that art in favour of intangible and uncrafted faith. The poet-priest Gerard Manley Hopkins used to destroy his poems, fearing they represented too heavy an intrusion of the ego over spiritual surrender. Tavener's mysticism might suggest that musical innovation – individuality, as it were – is curtailed, so that eternal verities are left uncluttered. Yet his music perpetually wavers between the simple and the complex, the direct and the suggested, the basic and the crafted.

Listen, though, to the earlier Taverner's *Misa Gloria tibi Trinitas*. There is the same pull between individuality and withdrawal into anonymity. Two strands run through the work. One is that of long, sweeping, simple melodies and lines that stretch along each whole section. The steady pace and focus of his music, like that of Tallis, is a brave contrast to the rather more overtly ornamental choral music of mainland Europe. These English church pieces take their time. They start steady and continue steady. They flee ostentation in favour of focused devotion. Yet all along Taverner's work is constant variation and complexity – differing combinations of voices and counter-melodies, great emotional range, constant variations over the main line. It's as if the eternal is set in motion, while the temporal plays around it.

This, I think, is the defining characteristic of English church music. Listen to the sweeping, stately melodies in the Eton Choirbook. It's a unique ability to seem simple, yet

... and Repeat

One of the grimmest and most emotionally overwhelm-ing operas is *Peter Grimes* and one of the grimmest, most emotionally overwhelming moments in it is the orchestral Passacaglia, at the start of Act 3. Like most of us, I knew *Peter Grimes* from the Four Sea Interludes Benjamin Britten arranged as a concert piece not long after the legendarily tri-umphant 1945 premiere, which are now standard orchestral showpieces.

The Interludes, though increasingly familiar, have not lost their ability to sound raw and terrifying. And they lead us to the opera. Which is why, when I sat through a performance of *Peter Grimes* for the first time, I was not only troubled and overwhelmed by the energy by which this disturbing tale is told, but amazed that its most impressive orchestral moment, the Passacaglia, should not have been included in the more public showpiece suite of orchestral extracts Britten launched soon after.

The Passacaglia comes at a crux point in the opera. Grimes, having been responsible for the death of one apprentice, is now ostracised by the community, and the recipient of only one person's trust: he is about to lose the life of another child, and the trust of the only person he has any affection for, leading inevitably to his own downfall. As the storm gathers pace outside, Grimes shows brutality towards his charge, and loses any remaining sympathy from the audience. It's a morally bleak, ravaged world, and we're brought into it by the music of the Passacaglia. It feels like a slow, sombre march in the distance, with a deathly viola solo at the front. A simple staccato tune tapping out a ticking-away of all remaining hope. It feels admonitory, but not yet climactic. The feeling is of subdued emotion. Perhaps the tragedy is inevitable, and inevitability removes any edge. This sounds like ritual. But then, a flash of electricity, and the tapping pulses become much louder, and the simple viola theme roars in a full, shrieking arrangement for the whole string orchestra, sliding and wailing like demons. The taps become thuds, things seem to draw nearer, what was inevitable is now overbearing and immediate. As each subtle variation or modified repetition of the theme adds another layer to the increasing clamour and discord breaking across the orchestra, we hit the stark realisation: this is no ritual. No matter how inevitable the tragedy may have appeared, it's rooted in reality, the very real consequences of a man's chosen actions. The musical form of the Passacaglia, a looped ground-bass embroidered with harmonic counter-melodies and variations, uses the variation to subvert the repetition; it makes us feel the real world impinge on the ritualised form.

Maybe Britten felt this was all too ghastly to package in a suite of orchestral interludes. Or maybe he knew that the full impact of this moment was only truly felt when you had listened to the whole of the drama that had led up to it.

It's music that only fully breathes when heard in complete context. The other Sea Interludes are depictions and impressions – a storm, some church bells – whereas the Passacaglia here is something much more complex and messier, a broken life and a fractured community doomed by the sea.

I've always been intrigued by musical forms that feed off repetition. Passacaglias, canons, fugues, chaconnes. There's an amazingly powerful passacaglia in Shostakovich's First Violin Concerto, the whole of the third movement, that's one of the most dramatic things he wrote. We celebrate Bach's Chaconne at the end of his Second Partita for solo violin as possibly the summit of solo violin-writing. Pachelbel's Canon is one of the most recognisable pieces of music ever written. These repetitive forms have impact. They can be mesmerising.

The repeated pulse or theme must appeal to something basic within us. You'd think we were dealing with theory and academia here; what could, on paper, seem more coldly formulaic than a five-part fugue? And yet, anyone who has sat through a live recital of Bach's *Well-Tempered Clavier* would testify to the dazzling drama of the occasion. Intricate, yes, but intimate also, these pieces are more than abstract theory given notation. The formality becomes liberating. Depicting not emotion but pure form, they feel all the more heartfelt because of it. The constraints liberate.

I'm reminded of when I first heard classical music – when, as a kid, I wasn't particularly interested in what category of music I was listening to, or what theory it adopted. Tonal, atonal, neoclassical, romantic were all terms less interesting than the noises. Maybe, without any grounding in theory, we're drawn to the most theoretical of patterns and shapes in music, basic repetitions and variations, because we sense,

Mobile Phones Off

I cross a bridge on the way to an orchestral concert. The bridge is a masterpiece of engineering; a complex calculus worked out by centuries of human brains keeps it from collapsing. The slightest error in the mathematics and the whole engineering project would have culminated in very wet disaster.

I approach symphony concerts with this precarious model in mind. The orchestral concert can be a glorious thing, but if you stand back and examine its components, if you analyse the ridiculous patterns of human tradition and behaviour that occur once people enter a concert hall, the whole thing collapses under the weight of its imposed seriousness. Anyway, I arrive: and now I just have to switch my mobile off.

I have a recurring dream about symphony concerts, and that dream involves deep space. In the dream, scientists send rockets off to find intelligent life in the cosmos. They place a piece of classical music in the satellite's software, because classical music, in all its intangible purity, sums up to us the unique quality of our humanity that sets us apart from other life forms. We could send the aliens something grander: a sports stadium, for example, or Paris. But the cost would be prohibitive. And in my dream, the craft travels for billions of miles until it enters a distant star system. There, an advanced alien culture uses tiny electric listening nodules, located at the base of each one of their eleven legs, to listen to a digitally encoded snatch of a Rachmaninov symphony.

The aliens love the music so much they send a delegation to Earth to hear more Rachmaninov. A billion alien well-wishers tearfully wave the fleet off, crying from tear ducts in their stomach. The ship's powerful on-board computers detect a symphony concert in Britain that it can buy tickets for online. Light-years later, the ship lands and the aliens enter the concert hall. That's when my dream turns to night-mare. Apart from getting very odd looks from the rest of the audience, the aliens clearly don't know the first thing about concert-hall etiquette. They cheer when the conductor starts the music. They applaud after each instrument finishes a phrase. And they blow steam out of their arms. People are looking at them disapprovingly. The aliens suddenly feel ... alienated. They sense hostility and they express this sen-sation by howling a high-pitched electronic signal that sets off someone's mobile phone. Tempers fray, and an elderly gentleman kindly tells the aliens that they're spoiling the enjoyment of others ... but is swiftly silenced when all of England is destroyed in a thermonuclear attack from the mothership. The aliens leave, and, to be on the safe side, the UN bans all music for ever.

I'm now in the foyer. Like everyone else around me, I've only got about twenty minutes to collect my tickets, hand over my coat, buy a programme, decide whether my metab-olism will survive without anything to eat until ten o'clock, and if not, locate some soup of the day – or, worst-case scenario this – some black olive tapenade at five pounds fifty a serving, and still leave time to go to the toilet. If there are more than two of us, the chances of confusion and disaster multiply exponentially. Around me I can see stranded husbands using their mobiles to establish contact with their wives. One of them, like a crestfallen NASA scientist transmitting emergency call-pulses to his space probe, had decided the last chance is over. He'll have to go in on his own, abandoning his wife to the vast, hostile wastes of the Ladies.

And – as if to unsettle us further – and shake all concert-goers out of their complacent quest for inner harmony, the organisers have booked Jazz in the Foyer. 'Jazz in the Foyer' is one of those things, like Mickey Mouse or the Commonwealth Games, which I've never heard anyone express a positive appetite for. They're just there. No one seems to get any outward pleasure from Jazz in the Foyer, but we're happy to put up with it and assume that someone else is getting the benefit. If only we could harness Jazz in the Foyer for the good of mankind. It's a dream, and not one I believe I'll see fulfilled in my lifetime.

And suddenly, as we enter the auditorium, the atmosphere changes; the shrieking and panicking outside is replaced by murmuring, like crowds in a cathedral, as we take our seats.

Concerts are faintly religious in layout and tone. The platform stands empty like an altar, and the hush and reverence, coupled with my own Catholic upbringing, always come close to making me want to genuflect before I move along the row containing my seat. An announcement urges everyone to switch their phones off.

Here it's hard not to feel as if you're in a room of spiritual observance, where tradition takes over. Nothing need be explained, and most things are now forbidden. You cannot talk, smoke, use your mobile, eat sweets, clack your glasses case shut, sneeze, remove false limbs, whimper, cry, stab, hiccup, or cough. It's a room hoaching with suppression. I fully expect an announcement instructing everyone to breathe in – once, at the beginning of the concert – and wait until the interval before letting it out. At this stage, there isn't time to take in your neighbours. Later on, we'll get to know their every twitch and respiratory peculiarity, but for the moment, as the crowd hushes and the ceremony starts, there are enough strange wordless traditions to keep the mind occupied.

When the orchestra walk on, for example, to applause from the audience, why don't they acknowledge that applause with thank-yous, rather than sauntering over to their seats as if in yet another rehearsal? A few of them look up at us, and the suspicion forms that the orchestra are judging us, that *we* are *their* concert for tonight. The quieter we are, the better our performance. Last night, our bronchial presentation was abysmal. The entry of the hacking phlegm attack in Row S was out of all proportion to the more regulated coughing in the stalls. And how seventeen people in Row F managed to coordinate what amounted to a row-long Mexican sneeze is beyond the orchestra's understanding.

The applause grows rapturous. Why? Any aliens here tonight would grow confused. Why is the conductor getting all this approval when he's clearly *very* late? Everyone was on the point of starting just when he eventually turned up. He should be ashamed of himself, instead of giving it the big I Am.

This is the moment that never fails to surprise me at any concert: the fact that no one speaks to us. There are no welcomes or explanations. Our introduction to the music is compacted into programmed note form. We're left to pick our way through the musical argument unaided. It's why, if you've had no formal musical training, and if the music isn't grabbing or familiar throughout, a concert can be an intimidating experience.

Looking around me, why do I only spot members of the audience who reinforce this sudden collapse in my intellectual self-confidence? Those three people over there are nodding their heads along with the conductor, juddering to the beat with their bodies, shutting their eyes, and quite unconsciously mimicking the sweep of the baton with their right hands. They're immersed in every shape and twist of the sound. Why can't I be? As if to turn my fears to the stuff of nightmare, a man four down from me is following the music from his own score – a giant of a book that must've cost at least a hundred pounds – which is also its weight. I console myself that though he may be, cerebrally speaking, quite cocky, he's also very clearly on his own.

And so we come to the end of the first piece of the programme. If it's a new piece, there's polite applause. If it's a popular classic, there's also polite applause. Tradition dictates we mustn't go too wild so early on in a concert.

I think back to accounts of concerts given in Beethoven's day. An orchestral piece may have been followed by a solo of chamber work, and often a movement from a concerto or symphony would be played two or three times over; the number determined by the size of the audience's enthusiasm. Concerts then sounded like raucous marathons. But fun. I wonder why we've petrified proceedings into the form they take today, where emotional responses to the music have to be internalised, and all public displays conform to a rigid code. I suppress the desire to shout 'God Almighty, that was gorgeous!' as the conductor takes a bow.

There's now a hushed sense of anticipation for the concerto that will bring the first half to an end. By tradition, the soloist will be a former child prodigy from Eastern Europe. Last night, the audience was mesmerised by a four-year-old Ukrainian baritone. Tonight, we're expecting someone who's made that difficult transition to full adulthood, her gift intact as she enriches her impressive range with the benefits of mature experience. And this is signalled by her wearing a low-cut red dress. She shakes the conductor's hand. I don't know why, since surely they've not just met. And she starts to play ...

Five away from me, a lady is watching her fingering through an expensive-looking monocular attached to the left lens of her glasses. Across the hall, in the cheap seats behind the orchestra, staring back at us, I see rows of young couples who've maybe come here on a whim, or a first serious date, buying last-minute standbys. They're not all wholeheartedly engaged. In one pair, She clearly suggested the concert and He went along with it. Now He does his best to feign interest, while trying to avoid looking like he's trapped in hell. He clearly has no interest in Rachmaninov.

The soloist looks to the conductor, the conductor back to the soloist. Someone behind me coughs three times, and the orchestra seem to take this as their cue to stop and leave the soloist playing on her own. Her Cadenza is brilliant. A man with a pad, three in front of me, writes down words to that effect. The boy in the cheap seats sees his girlfriend is enraptured, and starts reading the programme notes for something to do, before moving on to the wording on the soles of his shoes.

The Cadenza grows in complexity; the anticipation is palpable. The orchestra brings the music to a close. Crowds cheer! The boy rushes off to the bar so he can order a drink for his date, so she won't be rushed in the interval so they can get back in time so they won't miss a second of the next half.

And the soloist gets up and shakes hands with the conductor again, who introduces her to the leader of the orchestra, which seems a strange time for her to start networking, and she is presented with flowers and led off-stage, sweating like a boxer. The audience roar! She comes on again, then off. They roar further. They'll not be satisfied until she comes on then goes off again. The boy in the bar downs his first pint of Stella. She comes on then goes off again. The audience are satisfied. The noise now dips. She comes on again, having badly misjudged the audience's demands. She bows as the audience leave for the toilets. She vows never to come here again, even to give up her playing career. She goes off, and throws the flowers into a sand bucket.

Well, it's now the interval so I'm lifting my feet up off the floor so I can get carried along by the audience as they stampede out to the bar. The interval contains all the noise and mayhem I encountered in the foyer, but in one tenth of the space. To make it even more difficult, most of the bar has been taken up by the men who played Jazz in the Foyer, who've been camping here for the past hour. Penned in at the corner is the boy, who's summoning up enthusiasm for the second half by steadily getting drunk while surrounded by tenor saxophones. It's like a three-dimensional Hieronymus Bosch painting, but fortunately I don't have to plunge in because I calculate it's taken me ten minutes to get here, which means we're at the halfway point in the interval and it's time to head back.

It's a little known fact that if you examine till receipts of a hundred years of concerts in any region in Britain, you'll discover that only four people have managed to purchase any drinks.

As the symphony starts, it dawns on me that, just as in religious ceremony, it's perhaps wrong to search for a purely intellectual rationale. This is how we do live music. And while it may seem absurd, there are more than enough moments of magic and mystery to shake us out of our cynicism. Being at a concert, it strikes me, as the boy falls asleep four bars in and starts dribbling on his girlfriend's knee – though his dead neck makes his head nod in sleep (fortunately in time to the music, so his girlfriend thinks he's become totally engaged in the piece and makes a note to buy tickets for tomorrow night's concert, a Paul Hindemith programme (how he'll love it!)), and as the woman in front attaches a large mass-spectrometer to her glasses so she can examine in more detail the atomic make-up of the dot of ink on the third crotchet of the tuba player's sheet music, it strikes me that an orchestral concert is a drama, with the instruments as separate players. Very often, I find I don't need books and years of study to follow the structure of the music, if I concentrate on watching the orchestra. It's possible to see phrases leap from one side of the platform to another, to pass from strings to brass to woodwinds and back. Focusing on what's in front of you, the distractions in the corner of your eye disappear. You begin to see music act itself out.

We come to the end of the first movement, and one or two people clap. The rigid order of events asserts itself. The names and addresses of the troublemakers are passed on to the police, and after the concert they're arrested and taken away for clapping between movements. At their trial, the judge gives them a heavy sentence, saying it's necessary to make an example of scum like them.

And so, for the rest of the evening, I slip in and out of this realisation that attending a concert is all about watching music become human. It's not about perfection and abstraction. It's about fallibility and disorder. It's about moments where you feel totally captivated for a few seconds or so, before being reminded of where you are and who you're sitting with. It's not a free ride – you may have paid for the ticket, but you're expected to work. You must watch carefully where the music's going, and then you'll be rewarded.

Which is why, at the end of the concert, I sometimes think it rather spoils things when we shout for more. Shouting 'More! More!' is us saying to the orchestra, 'Work more! Work more for free!' They'd be perfectly entitled to shout back: 'Well, pay us more!' But they don't, and the conductor performs the ritual of walking off, then on again, and this time the audience gets it right and everyone's honour is satisfied.

But there's always that curious letdown at the end, as we leave the auditorium. If the concert has provided even one thrilling memory, I want to share it with everyone. So why isn't the building full of people hugging perfect strangers next to them, saying, 'Wasn't that wonderful? That bit where the clarinet suddenly came in with the phrase that started the strings – wasn't it simply great?'

But instead, people talk about where to go for buses and taxis, and late cafés. We all prefer to keep our emotional responses silent, like a congregation leaving Midnight Mass too embarrassed to talk about God.

Then, walking home across the bridge, I think maybe there's no need to talk about it. Whatever happened, happened, and maybe it'll happen next time too. The young couple stride towards a kebab van, and in the car park, two perfectly happy space aliens get back into their galactic cruiser and head for the Crab Nebula. As it takes off, the ship's ion-powered engines release a pulse of energy which causes every mobile phone in every concert throughout the world to start ringing, for ever.

Twice is Nice

Most of us can remember the first record we ever bought. Mine was Holst's *The Planets*, played by the Hallé Orchestra. I went out and bought it after hearing it at my first Musical Appreciation lesson at school. The teacher let the needle thud down onto the start of 'Mars', and my love of music started.

Our first record stays in the memory, but how many of us can remember the first piece of music we bought more than one recording of? Buying your first record is probably a youthful experience, but buying your first CD of a piece of music you've already got is more a middle-age rite of passage, like the transition from the teenage fad of putting posters up in the bedroom to the much more responsible act of hanging framed paintings in the front lounge.

I often think the intense comparison between different recordings, different critical interpretations, is something that passes me by, but then I stumble across recordings in which it is the particular interpretation I'm listening to that provides the key, the moment when the music starts to make sense, and when I start feeling particularly grateful for what those particular performers have done.

It happened to me recently with Bruckner. Being a long-time fan of Mahler, I've always felt I should like Bruckner. Indeed, I've spent the past twenty years listening to an awful lot of Bruckner, telling myself that I like him. And yet a niggling doubt has steadily rattled around in my head: why don't I thrill to Bruckner the way I do to Mahler or Wagner? Why am I prepared to give time, lots of time, to his symphonies, but why have I never come away feeling entirely satisfied? I seem to enjoy moments within them, but never the whole things themselves.

And then, a revelation from a recent performance: listening to Bernard Haitink at this summer's Proms conducting the Seventh Symphony. Hearing the slow movement, there was something about the pacing, the gradual but deliberate unfolding of the movement, that made me see that the satisfaction comes from hearing the long shape of the music reveal itself. I could hear the music make its structure known; there was no wilful flourish in the performance that distracted the listener from the memory of how the piece started, how it developed, and how it was concluded; instead, the shape, the code, was patiently but brilliantly laid out, and one was left knowing that there's a type of satisfaction to be gained from hearing a piece of music play with time and with your perception of its own length. I had previously been listening to bits and pieces of Bruckner; now I was being led through the whole. So I'm going out and buying Haitink conducting Bruckner, even though I've got all the symphonies already. For the same reason, I'm faithfully keeping up to date with John Eliot Gardner's Bach cantata cycle, since the clarity and spontaneity of his recordings have made me listen fresh and enthusiastically to these works, even though I've had many of them on CD for some time.

Speaking of Bach, I've always been a fan of Glenn Gould's piano recordings, but have often felt I was listening more to Gould than to Bach. Then, hearing a reissued 1970s recording of Sviatoslav Richter playing *The Well-Tempered Clavier*, I felt I was hearing the music directly and perfectly: what I'd heard in Haitink, that same sense of pace and patience as the structure of a large movement unfolds, is captured here in this more intimate form.

These magical performances don't render everybody else's interpretations useless. If anything, they make me want to go back and hear them again. It's been my experience that the key interpretations unlock and explain for me the meaning of the music, but that once this has been understood it's suddenly much more interesting to hear what others have done differently. So, I still listen to Glenn Gould playing Bach, enjoying the recording for its Glenn Gould-ness as much as its Bach-ness.

It was Gould, after all, who explained Haydn to me. I have a Columbia recording of Gould playing Haydn's Keyboard Sonata No. 48. The opening movement sounds like an idiosyncratic piece of improvised jazz. It's wilful and eccentric, but it made me realise why I like Haydn so much. He's so unpredictable. His music moves in an idiosyncratic way. You can't work out how a movement will end from how it starts. Now the Gould recording has made me see this. I enjoy playing this guessing game with all of Haydn's music, off any recording. That's the mark of a great performance: it augments rather than diminishes other interpretations.

In Sequence

The abundance of budget-price box sets of CDs now means there is no excuse for not being able to explore a favoured composer in depth. For me, this has led to the occasional spontaneous listening festival of a complete cycle; the chance, as the days go by, to hear all of, say, Bruckner's symphonies in chronological order. The trouble is, I don't know whether such an indulgence raises more questions than provides satisfactory answers.

For example, listening to the Mahler cycle of nine symphonies and the *Adagio* from the Tenth, conducted by Klaus Tennstedt, I was surprised by how late on in the cycle the distinctive Mahlerian voice began to emerge. What I mean by this is that unmistakably Mahlerian sound, a controlled, creative angst, that we would automatically associate with the composer and in which he seems more sure of himself and of his distinctive contribution to orchestral composition. The totally Mahlerian moment, to me, didn't seem to happen until the Fifth Symphony, and becomes at its most confident across the central triptych of Symphonies Nos 5, 6 and 7 (all of them, it's interesting to note, the most traditionally structured, and purely orchestral, of Mahler's symphonies). The central of these three, the Sixth, seems the most consistently confident, where no movement seems too long or too short, where what Mahler has to say is perfectly expressed.

That's not to say that the four symphonies at the beginning of the cycle are without their own bursts of originality. They are idiosyncratic works, pushing and straining at the symphonic form to see what happens, but the cumulative effect of listening to them is to hear someone courageously but also waywardly lashing out with orchestral sound, but unsure of where the result might lead. They're bold but uncontrolled. And then in Nos 5, 6 and 7 we arrive at the authentic, confident voice. By Symphonies Nos 9 and 10 we hear that voice mature, the sound of Mahler taking on fresh horizons, wandering into uncharted territory again but this time confident in his ability to preserve its distinctive sound. As the Tenth Symphony *Adagio* comes to a halt, I'm left feeling exhilarated but also frustrated; no sooner do new, exciting sounds emerge than they are silenced for ever.

Listening to a recent box set of all of Richard Strauss's orchestral music, admiring the colour and adventure but detecting no real progression, no development of a Strauss 'voice' that seems greater later than it does at the beginning, I was reminded of the remark someone made comparing Mahler and Strauss: noting Mahler died in his fifties and Strauss in his eighties, he asked us to imagine what twentieth-century music might have been like if it had been the other way around! The completist listen does that: makes you wonder, what if . . .? So, a recently issued, budget-priced box set of twenty-two CDs of Stravinsky's music, all conducted by the composer, posed similar questions. One is left at the end marvelling at Stravinsky's invention, but also wondering, was that mid-career neoclassical phase really worth it? Does the music from that period throw up the same sustained shock and surprise Stravinsky produced in abundance at the beginning and end of his career? It's good to have it but, heard next to what came before and after, it seems somehow to stall the dazzling progression.

I had a totally different, and completely unexpected, experience listening to Shostakovich's fifteen symphonies in quick sequence. The rarely heard Symphonies Nos 1, 2 and 3 seem strange; quirky, uncomfortable, uncompromising. The Fourth is challenging. And then, as we get into the more familiar territory of the Fifth, a thought began to form: we know that the Fifth was Shostakovich's attempt to rehabilitate himself with the Soviet authorities, to produce – his own words – an artist's 'response to just criticism'. Could it be that Shostakovich's true voice was what was uttered in his first four symphonies? That what he produced from the Fifth onwards was a public adaptation of that voice, not the real thing itself, but one conscious of the need to restrain the radical, even avant-garde urge? As I listen on through the rest of the cycle, I hear great symphonies (the Eighth and particularly the Tenth) but I also hear a repetitive bluster, a violent and sometimes comic savagery that seems born out of a deep frustration. I don't know how subjective and fantastical my supposition is, but hearing those first four symphonies again, I can't help but hear what Shostakovich wanted to be.

There's no answer, of course, so I'm left wondering, is it better to put all these troubling questions back in their box?

SKIN DEEP

Opera is both deeply serious and potentially ridiculous, so when asked to write one, what other answer could I possibly give?

If somebody asked you to write an opera you would, wouldn't you? Especially if that someone had the resources to put it on. I don't think you even have to be an opera buff, or a committed expert on the last three hundred years of musical drama, to leap at the chance to do something quite so absurd. A few years back, I was minding my own business when the composer David Sawer and the theatre and opera director Richard Jones approached me from nowhere and asked if I wanted to write the libretto of an opera. Not just any opera, but one that was actually going to happen. This wasn't mere idle speculation but solid commercial risk. Opera North, along with Austria's Bregenz Festival and the Royal Danish Opera, had commissioned David to compose another opera, in follow-up to his *From Morning to Midnight* at ENO in 2001. They were serious.

Fortunately, they weren't so serious about the content. David had decided he wanted to do a comic opera, more an operetta, and on a potentially stupid subject: cosmetic surgery. This instantly appealed. Cosmetic surgery seems to me the inevitable demented conclusion of all the impositions our culture imposes on us to look good, be cool and act in tune with the times. I've had a lifelong gripe about the tyranny of fashion. As a teenager I wore cardigans and slippers almost as an act of rebellion against the drip-feed of posters and gloss telling us what to wear and how to wear it. I say rebellion, though that's too strong a word to describe my utter, utter uninterest in what the clothing experts who think they govern us order us to put on. It's a concerted act of bullying, in which those who are too old, too knobbly, too bald, too chubby, too pale or too poor are made to feel like they don't belong to the predominant species unless they make an attempt to accessorise. What you do to your lips, your breasts or your backside can suddenly complement your hairstyle or your handbag.

As you can see, it didn't take much to get me started. Meeting up with David and Richard saw the pace become unstoppable. Soon we were concocting a plot about face swaps, people falling in love with their own post-op reflections, celebrities hoping for the ultimate cosmetic overhaul and the perennial search for inner beauty. All our admiration and consternation with the best, and silliest, plots in opera came tumbling out. Opera is at once the most serious and yet the most potentially ridiculous of art forms, and I've always felt you can only make an opera work if you not only take it seriously but are also perpetually aware of the pitfalls of absurdity into which it can collapse. It is, after all, larger-than-life individuals choosing to sing about their experiences in front of a paying public: there's so much about that which could either work brilliantly or just look plain weird. My (limited) experience as an opera-goer has been of someone nervous at the start of the evening, worried about what's about to happen. Many times I've been thrilled as soaring music, great stagecraft and marvellous colour all coalesce into a live event that simply cannot be replicated.

But frequently too I've seen the whole edifice come crashing down because something, usually indefinable, isn't quite right, and on those occasions, though there are great moments, the whole significantly refuses to be greater than the sum of its parts.

There's no telling what will happen. That's why one of my greatest musical memories is Wagner's *Tristan and Isolde* conducted by Reginald Goodall at ENO in 1984, and one of my worst is Wagner's *The Valkryie* at ENO twenty years later. One had me stilled and riveted to my seat, the other had me leaving at the first moment I could, and going to the cinema instead. I'm sure there was very little Wagner could do about it.

That's the risk we take with opera. It's what makes it the most precarious, potentially awful, but also potentially intoxicating, night out.

Which is why you need to hear opera live. Can a recording ever regenerate the sheer potential for disaster that a live night at the opera ushers in? There is always something strange in hearing huge, charismatic performers belt their lungs out into a sensitive microphone. Just as TV cameras can make an opera singer's exaggerated movements – movements meant to be seen from the back of a hall – seem hammy, so too does the audio recording all too often make an opera sound unnatural, a warble, a background wall of sound, rather than the amazing noise it can generate in a large auditorium. No, all that potential demands to be unleashed physically in front of you.

So, for all these reasons, and with all these fears and trepidations, I agreed to do it. Wouldn't you?

Skin Deep

Operetta in Three Acts (2006–8)
Music by David Sawer
Libretto by Armando Iannucci

CHARACTERS

Doktor Hermann Needlemeier,
plastic surgeon   *baritone*
Lania, his wife   *soprano*
Donna, his receptionist   *mezzo-soprano*
Elsa, his daughter   *soprano*
Robert, her boyfriend   *tenor*
Luke Pollock, a Hollywood actor   *bass-baritone*
Susannah Dangerfield,
a news reporter   *speaking role*

CHORUS *is divided into two in Acts One & Two.*
Clinic Staff (12 voices)   *soprano 1, 2, 3 & 4*
                                       alto 1 & 2
                                       tenor 1 & 2
                                       baritone 1 & 2
                                       bass 1 & 2

Villagers (24 voices)   *6 soprano, 6 alto, 6*
                                       tenor, 6 bass

solo parts within Villagers chorus

Solo	*1 soprano*
Quartet	*2 soprano, 2 alto*
Quartet	*2 tenor, 2 baritone*
Duet	*2 bass*

Chorus *sings as one SATB chorus (36 voices) in Act Three, with the following solo parts:*

Donnalike	*alto*
Robertalike One	*bass*
Robertalike Two	*baritone*

ACT ONE

No. 1
Overture

> *Some snow-covered Swiss slopes. Donna,*
> *receptionist at the Needlemeier Clinic, has just*
> *been injured skiing. Her face appears bloodied*
> *and gashed. Doktor Needlemeier is seen leaving*
> *his wife, Lania, to come over and tend to her. He*
> *organises the villagers to help him move her gently*
> *away from the scene of the accident.*

No. 2
Chorus

> *Morning at the Needlemeier Clinic, a chic and*
> *expensive plastic surgery clinic high up in the Swiss*
> *mountains, run by Doktor Needlemeier.*
> *   The clinic staff busy themselves on and off*
> *stage, getting on with the work of the day.*

Sometimes Donna is alone, other times the stage is crowded with staff as the clinic prepares to open.

CLINIC STAFF
    Liposuction
    Skin abrasion
    Buccal fattening
    Silical shaping

    Chin-bone wiring
    Mucosal plumping
    Nasal grafting
    Cranial hoisting

    Eyebrow lowering
    Earlobe pumping
    Cheek-bone shattering
    Jaw-hinge tightening

    Chemical peeling
    Mastopic patching
    Dermal scraping
    Platysmic slicing

    With craniopic expansion
    We stretch what's gone slack
    Apply fibril injections
    To tighten the skin sack

    We can patch over
    The unsightliest rashes

Use cannular cement
To minimise gashes

We do dermabrasion
And blepharoplasty
Use the best creams
On scars gone nasty

Incision, revision
Depilation, crenulation
Removal, insertion

And for men
We forgot to mention
We do penis—

DONNA
Penis—

CLINIC STAFF
—extension

No. 3
Solo & Chorus

> *At the reception desk, a phone line is very busy
> this morning. Donna repeatedly answers the calls.
> She has a very visible gash on her face, from the
> accident.*

DONNA

The Needlemeier Clinic
Putting right what Nature got wrong
Donna speaking
We'll keep your scar-line neat
Your attendance discreet

Phone line rings and Donna answers

Needlemeier Clinic. How can I help you?
We'll make your stay here pleasant
For an advance payment

Phone line rings and Donna answers

Donna speaking, putting right what Nature got
　　wrong
That's normal after a face lift
You'll find your hands don't match
They can be re-righted with chemical peeling
I'll book you in for a caustic scratch

Phone line rings and Donna answers

No, you'll find the hair never moults

Phone line rings and Donna answers

Splendid
If you come tomorrow
We'll remove all the bolts

Two phone lines ring and Donna answers

Donna, can you hang on?

lifts up phone two

Hello, Needlemeier's
I won't keep you long

back to phone one

Yes, you'd like a Botox injection

phone two

Oh, you think it's got an infection?

phone one

Yes, we'll put you down for next week

phone two

Why, of course, they shouldn't leak

phone one

Are you happy to pay by credit card?

phone two

Are you worried it's gone hard?

phone one

Splendid, we'll see you the third of May

phone two

No, the soreness should have gone away

phone three

Sorry, Ma'am, je ne parle pas Français

phone one

A pleasure Madam. Have a nice day

phone two

Not you Madam, come in right away

phone three

Sorry, at this stage, all you can do is pray.

Phone line rings and Donna answers

Donna at Needlemeier
Yes, you should soon be able to speak

Phone line rings and Donna answers

Yes, we can give you a more flattering enhancement
  of the eyes and lips consistent with the natural
  layout of the face
In under a week

Phone line rings and Donna answers

It's Donna
No, we're full until spring

Phone line rings and Donna answers

Yes, we use a range of skin creams and herbal
  medicines based on holistic Chinese remedies
The Doktor learnt in Beijing

CLINIC STAFF
  Trust Doktor Needlemeier
  He's done it to us
  No praise is higher

Phone line rings and Donna answers

DONNA
  No, the breasts cannot be punctured
  Ruptured or crushed

Phone line rings and Donna answers

Can you hold? I'm a little bit rushed

Phone line rings and Donna answers

No they can't be oozing
What cream are you using?
How much are you losing?

CLINIC STAFF
He reduced our backsides
By over a half
Reset our teeth
Prettified our laugh

SOLO BARITONE
I had protruding veins
He removed them without much pain

SOLO SOPRANO
I had unsightly hair
Now it isn't there

CHORUS
Trust Doktor Needlemeier
He's done it to us
No praise is higher

Phone lines ring and Donna answers

DONNA
It's all pretty relaxing
Even the anal waxing.

CLINIC STAFF
> Higher, higher

ROBERT *(offstage)*
> Yodelayeehoo!

> *Phone lines ring and Donna answers*

DONNA
> Oh, sorry, didn't I mention?
> He's gone to a cleft-palate convention

No. 4
Dialogue

> *Robert, a local village lad, is delivering chemicals.*
> *He arrives in dispatch-rider gear, with a large*
> *box full of glass bottles, and interesting-looking*
> *packages of powders and creams.*

ROBERT *(distracting Donna on the phone)*
> Yodelayeehoo!

DONNA
> *Ssssh, Robert, I'm on the phone.*

ROBERT *(shouts)*
> *Sorry!*

DONNA *(down phone)*
> No, Madam. The silicone is only partially solid. They
> should still be able to—

ROBERT *(across to phone)*
> Wobble.

DONNA *(down phone)*
> . . . move . . .

ROBERT *(across to the phone)*
> . . . like Turkish Delight . . .

DONNA *(down phone)*
> . . . naturally. Goodbye.

ROBERT
> Bye bye!

> *(phone down)*

DONNA *(to Robert)*
> Stop clattering about like a gibbon. I was just telling
> someone this is the most tranquil place in Europe to come
> and have her breasts inflated.

ROBERT
> Hardly tranquil. Every time I bring a delivery I can hear
> half a dozen millionaires screaming their noses haven't set.

> *(Looks in mirror and makes a false scream of
> horror)*

Aaargh! My nostrils are loose!

DONNA

Sssshhh!

ROBERT

Only joking. My nose is perfect.

DONNA

Does Elsa think you're perfect? Every little bit of you?

ROBERT

Listen, waffle-cheeks: Elsa's happy to marry me as I am.

DONNA

Her father isn't. Needlemeier won't let you anywhere near his daughter until he's got you just right. So don't get cocky, little delivery boy.

ROBERT

Oh, cheer up. You're busier than you've ever been. You should have a smile on.

   (points to the gash on Donna's face)

At a certain angle it does look like a smile.

DONNA *(pointing to it herself)*
How would you like it if somebody snowboarded across your face?

ROBERT

You know, this close, I can see where they did their emergency stop.

(Donna lunges at him with a sharp implement)

DONNA

Can I book you in for a 'treatment'?

(pushes knife to skin)

ROBERT

Hey, good knife skills. Has Needlemeier been teaching you nights?

(Donna puts knife down. She knows this is a sensitive subject)
(phone rings)

DONNA

Herr Doktor will be over in a minute. Have you got the deliveries?

ROBERT

Eight tubs of pure alcohol
In batches of ten mill

DONNA

To deaden the pain
From Herr Doktor's drill

ROBERT

    Nine sacks of collagen
    And this curious thing?

DONNA

    It's a power chisel
    To pierce knotted skin

ROBERT

    Six flasks of botulism
    And, my God, what's that?

DONNA

    Just a little mallet
    To hit clawed toes flat

ROBERT

    Ugh, six bits of animal parts
    Why are they in this box?

DONNA

    To make tear-ducts from tendons
    Snipped from the legs of a fox

ROBERT

    Thank God I'm handsome
    I think I feel sick
    This is ungodly
    Take this stuff, quick!
    Demerol
    Propanol
    Iodine

Triethylene
Bovine Collagen
Glycolic Pathogen
Copper Peptide
Alpha Hydroxide
Carbon Dioxide
Lactic Malcide
And if you still look ugly
There's always Cyanide

> *Donna leaves with some of the bottles. Elsa,*
> *Needlemeier's daughter, emerges from behind a*
> *mirror. Robert can't see her.*

ELSA *(surprising him from behind)*
    Boo!

No. 5
Duet

ROBERT
    Elsa! Watch out. That's expensive stuff.

ELSA
    Robert, you know I can afford to pay for any damage.

BOTH *(kissing)*
    Mm-Mm
    Mm-Mm-Mm

ELSA

Oh Robert, Robert, I missed you last night.

ROBERT *(holding a mirror up in front of Elsa, so Elsa can see his reflection in it)*
I'm not surprised. A face like yours just cries out for a face like mine next to it.

BOTH *(kissing)*
Mm-Mm
Mm-Mm-Mm
Mm-Mm-Mm-Mm

ELSA

Robert! Not here, remember!

ROBERT

Sorry. Forgot you have to watch your back here – and your nose. Close your eyes for a second and your father will chop two inches off it.

ELSA

He'd put two inches elsewhere if I wrote him a cheque.

ROBERT

Shhsshh!
Do you promise that
After our wedding day
We won't need to whisper
Everything we say?

ELSA

> I do, I do, I do
> But that day will only come
> When you have the perfect nose and bum

ROBERT

> *How can mine compete with yours?*

ELSA

> *But these are my father's work. Let him work on you.*

ROBERT

> No, no, never
> I will not let your father
> Circumcise my face
> Peel away my cheeks
> Or slice a tender place

ELSA

> One day when you're old
> And can't get it up
> You'll quite happily pay
> For a resurrecting op

ROBERT

> No, Elsa, no!

ELSA

> *Just some work on the ears.*

(Elsa reveals a full-length photo of Robert, and is drawing on it. There are already stitch-marks all over the face and limbs)

ROBERT

My ears?

(Robert checks himself in a mirror)

ELSA

Slightly big – an adjustment to the lips.

ROBERT

My lips?

ELSA

Slightly jugged – some work on the stomach.

ROBERT

My stomach?

ELSA

Too extended – and a bit off your butt.

ROBERT

My butt?
But, but –
You said you adored
Every bit of me

ELSA

>I do, I do, I do
>I adore and I love you
>I love you, love you
>But you have fatty wrists

ROBERT

>Why do these demands persist?

ELSA

>Your chin hangs like a chicken

ROBERT

>No, I won't listen

ELSA

>Your nose could be straight

ROBERT

>*Why do you want what I haven't got? Why don't you love me?*

ELSA

>Oh but I do love you
>My love is like a pearl
>Compact and pure
>But if you were perfect
>My love would be more
>My love would grow mighty
>Breach Earth in its span
>Why be content with a pearl
>When you can have the moon?

ROBERT

>Then I will do this
>All I have is yours

ELSA

>You agree to small changes?

ROBERT

>I do, I do, I do

ELSA

>I've drawn on your photo
>Where you can be improved
>Smooth out the jaw-line
>The ears pushed back
>Stop the jowls sagging
>And take up the slack

ROBERT

>I am all yours

ELSA

>You agree?

Elsa pulls out a contract and pen.

ROBERT

>I do

ELSA

>To a nose job and pin-back?

ROBERT

I do

ELSA

To a tummy tuck and a jaw-crack?

ROBERT

I do

ELSA

Do you swear?

ROBERT

I do

ELSA

To a review every third year?

ROBERT

I do

ELSA

And to a penis extension?

ROBERT

I do, I do, I do

As they exit, Robert signs the contract.

No. 6a
Solo

> *There are several operating theatres at the back of*
> *the clinic, each one with a photo of the patient's*
> *face above the doorway. Needlemeier comes in*
> *and out of them, wearing an increasingly bloodied*
> *gown. It's clear that he's performing several*
> *operations at once, like a chess Grand Master*
> *taking on a multitude of opponents. He comes out*
> *to get wiped down and have a drink, while getting*
> *rid of bloodied swabs.*

NEEDLEMEIER

When a man's kept awake at night
By the smell of age in his breath
And a woman's fingers claw in the dark
At chins that sag with death
They both come crying to me

When she's too afraid to smile
For the thousand cracks her smile sets free
When naked he looks to the ground
And all he can see is him all round
The ground he cannot see
But him all around
A tumbling mound
They all come dying to me

> *A photo of Robert's face is put up above the*
> *doorway, ready for his operation.*

No. 6b
Duet

> *While the clinic reception area is briefly quiet,*
> *Needlemeier creeps slowly near Donna.*

NEEDLEMEIER
> *Is she here yet?*

DONNA
> *No, it's safe to talk.*

NEEDLEMEIER
> Donna
> I wish I could kiss you

DONNA
> Doktor
> I wish I could hold you

NEEDLEMEIER
> I wish I could have you

BOTH
> I want to be close to you

DONNA
> Yet, when I see your wife
> I feel so far

NEEDLEMEIER

    Yet, when I come near you
    I see your scar

DONNA

    This gash is a bar in a cage
    That each day restricts me
    From your bed

NEEDLEMEIER

    I'd sing a song to your beauty
    Each morning and night
    But for your wound
    You will be ugly no more

> *Needlemeier reveals a photograph of Donna's
> gashed face. He starts drawing chalk marks over
> it. Meantime, a gowned-up and nervous-looking
> Robert is seen in the background, going into the
> operating theatre marked out with a photo of his
> face above the doorway.*

    Are you ready?

DONNA

    I am ready

NEEDLEMEIER

    I'll turn an ugly duckling
    To a perfect dove
    Your face the perfect mirror
    For my perfect love

BOTH

    Then I can kiss you
    Then I can hold you

DONNA

    Then I can have you

NEEDLEMEIER

    Then I can mould you

NEEDLEMEIER / DONNA

    Then I'll be close to you
    All your imperfections / All my imperfections
    I'll put right / You'll put right
    With the arrival of our guest tonight

NEEDLEMEIER

    Your face

DONNA

    My face

NEEDLEMEIER

    Your cheeks

DONNA

    My cheeks

NEEDLEMEIER

    Your lips

DONNA

   My lips

NEEDLEMEIER

   Put me off

DONNA

   Put you off

NEEDLEMEIER

   So your face

DONNA

   So my face

NEEDLEMEIER

   Must come off

DONNA

   Must come off?

     Needlemeier holds up the photo of Donna so she
     can see what he's drawn on it. He's marked a large
     cross though her face and indicated that the whole
     thing will be removed.

No. 6c
Operation conducted by Puppets

> *While Needlemeier disappears into the operating theatre a puppet version of Robert's operation is carried out.*

No. 7a
Solo

> *Needlemeier emerges from the operating theatre with a plastic container full of bits of flesh.*

NEEDLEMEIER

I've removed fat from the lips
Of six Swiss philosophers
I gave a long-haired rock star
Most of his longest locks
I've polished up the face
Of an Italian prime minister
He still hasn't paid me
So I keep his old cheeks in a box
For I am Doktor Needlemeier
And I put right what Nature got wrong

I thickened the knees of a pope
To kneel more piously in prayer
I improved the smile of a diva
To match her wonderful song.
I remove all your blotches and flaws
Why? Not why? Just because.

I reduce the large and the long
For I am Doktor Needlemeier
Who puts right what you've got wrong

I've smoothed out the skins
Of three French presidents
And used the spare to repair
A hump on an English prince
His mother bargained with me
On the day he was born:
'Take my crown and my diamonds,
Have my orb when the lump is gone'
For I am Doktor Needlemeier
Who puts right what you've got wrong

And I was visited once by a woman
A beauty they said no man could perfect
Until I gave her a close inspection
And that perfect claim was wrecked
Her left eyelid drooped
A millimetre more than the right
She would be an abomination
Unless I performed that night
She happily paid me a fortune
Now her lids are the talk of Bonn
She said thank you Doktor Needlemeier
For putting right what Nature got wrong

Phone line rings.

DONNA *(on phone)*
> *Needlemeier's, Donna speaking.*
> *Has he left LA? Yes, we're ready, we've had Hollywood*
> *actors before, you know. Yes, his room's been painted his*
> *favourite colour. As has everything he can see from his*
> *window.*

No. 7b
Duet

NEEDLEMEIER
> *Is he here yet?*

DONNA
> *He'll be here by nightfall.*

NEEDLEMEIER
> *Another four hours.*

BOTH
> Prepare for Luke Pollock
> The world's most famous actor
> Playing his greatest part:
> Possessor of charisma

> > *They pull down a full-length photo of Hollywood*
> > *superstar Luke Pollock.*

NEEDLEMEIER
> And soon, my ugly duckling
> Flies free from its cage

DONNA

    And soon, my great Doktor,
    We both will never age

NEEDLEMEIER

    One last procedure

DONNA

    One more revision

NEEDLEMEIER

    Take one of his bollocks

DONNA

    Make one more incision

> *Instead of marking up Pollock's face on the photo,*
> *Donna puts a chalk mark and arrow pointing to*
> *one of his testicles.*

BOTH

    All life's imperfections we'll put right
    With the part we cut from him tonight

NEEDLEMEIER

    Your lips

DONNA

    My lips

NEEDLEMEIER

    Your cheeks

DONNA

My cheeks

NEEDLEMEIER

Your face

DONNA

My face

NEEDLEMEIER

I will restore

DONNA

I will adore

NEEDLEMEIER

So your lips

DONNA

My lips

NEEDLEMEIER

So your cheeks

DONNA

My cheeks

NEEDLEMEIER

So your face

DONNA

My face

NEEDLEMEIER

Will be like before

DONNA

Will age no more

No. 7c
Solo

> *Needlemeier puts his bucket of removed body fat*
> *on a trolley with other similar buckets, and wheels*
> *it across to a private room.*

NEEDLEMEIER

And all the time I've been sluicing
The flabby rumps of the famous
Bolting, burning and slicing
The arid bones of the rich

> *He reveals the side of a large vat, into which he*
> *starts pouring the slops.*

Keeping these off-cuts
For a better purpose
Their skins and their fat
And all they think surplus
I've placed in a vat
To boil and reduce
To the stock of life
A compact DNA

To keep me strong
For tonight, tonight
I will put right
What the infallible God has got wrong

No. 8
Mute Dance with Chorus

> *Lania emerges from the rear of the stage. Beautiful*
> *but silent. The staff administer last-minute polishes*
> *to the mirrors. As they finish up, Lania walks slowly*
> *forward, catching her reflection in the mirrors.*

CLINIC STAFF
Hush, the time is ready
Hush, she comes towards us
Hush, can we hear her?
Hush, dumb beauty

As age tries to shrivel us
And dreams look impossible
Lania is made lovelier
By Needlemeier's scalpel

On this day every year
The birthday of his wife
Herr Doktor puts her under
And purifies with his knife

And Lania grows radiant
Her youth in fuller bloom

Needlemeier rekindles
The dawn of bride and groom

Hush
Will she sing tonight?
Hush

> Lania turns to them but says nothing. She leaves
> through a doorway with a picture of her face
> above it.

No. 9
Chorus & Solo

> Susannah Dangerfield emerges from the chorus of
> staff members. She's a news reporter in disguise.
> She pulls out a microphone and addresses a
> camera that emerges from the dark.

SUSANNAH DANGERFIELD

*Hi, this is Susannah Dangerfield, undercover for Global.
Glamour BizzBuzz. I'm bringing you exclusive pictures
from the world-famous Needlemeier Clinic at the cosmetic
face-fest of the year. Tonight, skilled scalpel supremo
Doktor Hermann Needlemeier is throwing a birthday
party for his increasingly gorgeous wife Lania. All his
clients are attending. Yes, it's a night of chin-wagging for
people whose chins were previously sagging.*

> (She points to the full-length poster of Luke Pollock)

Among those letting their hair down and pinning their
cheeks back is an extra-special guest, because Oscar-
winning actor Luke Pollock is in town. Amazingly,
though, the world's biggest publicity-seeker is in disguise.
Maybe he's talking to Needlemeier about losing those love
handles he's recently been carrying around. If so, Luke
Pollock could be setting another first: an actor who wants
bits of him to end up on the cutting-room floor.

Whatever happens, there'll be full coverage of the way
of all flesh from me, Susannah Dangerfield, reporting for
Global.Glamour BizzBuzz.

> (Susannah puts away the microphone and tries
> to blend in with the staff once again. She has a
> notebook, and tries writing down what they say. A
> Chorus of Ointments and Creams perform a small
> song and dance.)

CLINIC STAFF

Apply, smear, soothe
Rub, refresh, remove
Massage 'til smooth
These creams will wipe away your years

SUSANNAH

. . . *years*

CLINIC STAFF

Silky, sanitising
Milky, moisturising
Eggy, energising
These creams will wipe away your fears

SUSANNAH
... will wipe away your fears

No. 10
Interlude under Anaesthetic

In the darkness, Lania has her operation.

No. 11
Duet

As the lights come up, we see Robert regaining
consciousness after his own surgery. He's laid out
on a trolley; Elsa is by his side.

ROBERT
Has it worked?

ELSA
Have you no faith?

ROBERT
Hand me the mirror

ELSA
See for yourself

Robert starts gazing longingly – too longingly – at
his reflection.

ROBERT

Such a vision of beauty

ELSA

With beauty comes wealth

> *Robert gets off the trolley and stands in front of a*
> *full-length mirror.*

ROBERT

Such jaunty features

ELSA

So tender a chin

ROBERT

So perfect the nose

ELSA

So smooth the skin

ROBERT

And down here I feel it

ELSA

Robert—

ROBERT

I'm no longer tiny

ELSA

> — I know
> Large ...

ROBERT

> ... to Extra-Large below

ELSA / ROBERT

> Your / My eyes are like almonds
> Your / My cheeks apple red
> Your / My lips full but manly

ROBERT

> I am a success

ELSA

> Let's go to get wed

ROBERT

> The scales from my eyes
> Have come undone
> I see the truth now
> I am the sun

ELSA

> Let's go to get wed

> *Elsa is now trying to pull him away from the
> mirror; Robert is resisting.*

ROBERT

>Like Christ fresh arisen
Just given all his blood
So I'm newly fashioned
Fresh Adam from mud

ELSA

>Let's go to get wed

ROBERT

>But Eve am I also
For in my face
Sits the perfect vision
Of feminine grace

ELSA

>Let's go to bed

ROBERT

>No
I now cleave to no one
Only myself I embrace
I am my own lover
Betrothed to my face

ELSA

>Let's go to bed

ROBERT

>My love, I cannot love you
Now I see how much more

I need me for my happiness
It's me I adore

ELSA

You need some rest
Please go to bed

ROBERT

In bed I'll embrace me
And kiss my own form
And sleep with this mirror
To greet me in the morn
It's me that I'll wed

They leave, Robert pulling the mirror behind him.

ACT TWO

*Evening of the same day. The clinic has been made
ready for a grand party. Drinks are served from
a bar area near the reception desk. The theme
of the party is 'Looking Good, Feeling Great!'
Needlemeier's vat is now more visible.*

No. 12a
Chorus

VILLAGERS *(offstage)*
 Sing praise!
 Sing praise!
 Sing praise!
 To Needlemeier sing praise!

 Sing of new faces
 Unravelled tonight
 Sing of the ugly
 He now puts right

Sing praise!
Sing praise!

No. 12b
Ballet of Transplant Organs

> *Organs removed from surgery appear and perform a dance.*

No. 13

CHORUS OF VILLAGERS
A new day is dawning
For those scared of yawning
It's the end of the reign
Of the varicose vein
Sing praise!
To Needlemeier!

SUSANNAH
What has he done?

> *(she realises that others are looking at her with surprise)*

> *(joining in the singing)*

Sing of what he's done!

VILLAGERS

Sing praise!

SUSANNAH

Sing praise!

DUET OF VILLAGERS

He strengthened the lungs of a singer
Who wanted to reach a high C
He used skin from the arse of a rhino
And cells from a weightlifter's knee

QUARTET OF VILLAGERS

Ten racing drivers
Piled up in a horrible mix
Herr Doktor patched four of them
With bits from the other six
He stitched five abandoned toes
On a hand that was maimed
And carved out two new ears
From a tongue that wasn't claimed

DUET

Let's drink to Needlemeier!

NEEDLEMEIER *(to Susannah)*

Do you remember Su?

SUSANNAH

Su? Do I remember Su?
Of course I do. Do you?

WOMEN *(to Susannah)*
    Tell us the story of pretty Su

SUSANNAH *(caught out, to Quartet)*
    Over to you

QUARTET
    Su was a goodly maiden
    The goodliest that ever had been
    Born of the poorest parents
    The poorest the village had seen

VILLAGERS
    Poor Su

SUSANNAH
    So what did poor Su do?

QUARTET
    And so to free her parents
    From all this mire and muddle
    Su began to pursue
    A career as a supermodel

VILLAGERS
    Su, become a supermodel?
    What twaddle!
    For the story goes
    The story goes—

(to Susannah)

The story goes—

SUSANNAH *(to Solo)*
As everyone knows—

SOLO
Su had a bent nose

QUARTET
Yes, it's true
The thing about Su
Was that being a supermodel could never suit her
Because of her bent hooter

VILLAGERS
Su was fair and light-hearted
Gracious and respected
Su had a lot to shout about
Apart from her crooked snout

SUSANNAH
But tell us
Remind me
What did we do
For poor Su?

SOLO VILLAGER
We rallied round her
Raised all we could
Sold off our silver

Replaced lead roofs with wood
Made a small fortune
And left more in our will
So Su could afford
Needlemeier's skill

VILLAGERS
Good for Su!

SUSANNAH
Good for you!

QUARTET
Though poor, we're not dejected
For Su's conk has been corrected

SUSANNAH
Now Su's a rich supermodel
Let's express our joy in a yodel
Yodelayee-ooh!

No. 14
Solo

Another section of the party, away from the noise,
Elsa is fraught and alone.

ELSA *(upset, she starts removing mirrors to prevent Robert falling*
even deeper in love with his own image)
Look, look
My looks lie empty

My eyes all aglaze
My spirit departed
There's death on my face
Look, look
How these mirrors curse me
Reflecting my anguish
And blessing my Robert
With looks more languid
His looks that betray me
For they out-do me
But I can catch him
If I try to match him
Match his unequalled beauty
Made by my father
Who fashioned a diamond
From merest gold

*(Looking at her own reflection, Elsa starts fingering
her face, as if practising surgery on it)*

So shall I match him
With my father's knife
Cheek for cheek
Chin for chin
Eye for eye
Skin for skin
He'll look and he'll see me
Looking like him
And soon will my Robert
The love of a second Robert win

No. 15
Dialogue, Solo & Ensemble

> *Over at the main party area, Needlemeier has*
> *appeared from behind the vat.*

DONNA
> *How's the vat?*

NEEDLEMEIER
> *Quite a sight.*

DONNA
> *Thirteen tons of human fat boiled down to the size of a*
> *pint of milk.*

NEEDLEMEIER
> *Wonderful. The congealed genes of the rich, powerful and*
> *strong reducing away like a chicken stock. And now for*
> *the stock cube: a testicle from the most charismatic man*
> *in the world.*

DONNA
> *The final ingredient for the elixir of life.*

NEEDLEMEIER
> *Any news on Luke Pollock?*

SUSANNAH *(trying to listen, while making discreet notes)*
> *Pollock?*

DONNA

A flight from Hollywood landed this afternoon.

NEEDLEMEIER

Good. Prepare the executive suite. Was Pollock on board?

DONNA

No. But the jet contained his personal trainer, masseur, lunchtime chef and left- and right-hand manicurists.

NEEDLEMEIER

Oh. Prepare five more executive suites.

DONNA

But another flight landed not long after. It contained his evening chef and hair consultant.

NEEDLEMEIER

But no Luke Pollock?

SUSANNAH

Pollock?

DONNA

No, but I'm told he's never more than seven minutes away from his hair consultant. So he must be near by.

NEEDLEMEIER

Very well, prepare a couple of executive floors for them all.

DONNA *(just receiving a text message)*
> Herr Doktor, a fleet of cars has just pulled up outside.
> Security says the first car's got Pollock's bodyguards, and
> his bodyguards' pilates instructors. The second's got his
> evening chef's legal team. Behind it are Pollock's fourteen
> voice coaches, in a coach.

NEEDLEMEIER
> Right. Prepare everywhere. Designate the whole
> Accommodation Block an Executive Accommodation
> Block and prepare it. Christ, that egomaniacal actor's
> going to bankrupt me—

POLLOCK *(dressed as a villager, stepping from out the crowd)*
> I'm here already, Doktor.

NEEDLEMEIER
> Luke Pollock!

SUSANNAH
> Luke . . .!

> *(everyone turns and looks at her)*

> Look! A small goat eating a balloon.

> *(she points to the opposite end of the stage.*
> *Everyone looks over that way. She disappears into*
> *the crowd by the time they all turn round)*

POLLOCK

I arrived this morning. I hope you don't mind. I booked in
quietly. I can't stand fuss.

NEEDLEMEIER

So your fifteen publicists were telling me. But we were
very much looking forward to putting on a grand
welcome.

DONNA

The Doktor has planned a firework display and open-air
reception.

> *(Donna points to the doorway, and a gate leading*
> *out into the garden. Pollock suddenly recoils as she*
> *opens it)*

POLLOCK

Open? Open?!

SUSANNAH

He's feverish. Why does he fear the open?

POLLOCK

No, no. Not there.
Not in the open *air!*

SUSANNAH

No wonder he's agitated. This actor is agoraphobic.

POLLOCK

There might be a photographer, you understand. I'd prefer to keep things discreet.

NEEDLEMEIER

Of course. We wouldn't want the whole world to know about—

POLLOCK *(loudly, to the villagers)*

My small toe problem that needs correcting.

      (to Needlemeier)

You have the elixir?

NEEDLEMEIER *(presenting him with a bill to sign)*

Yes . . .

      (quietly to Donna and taking a cup)

. . . that's not the elixir?

DONNA *(quietly to Needlemeier)*

No – a very strong sleeping potion.

NEEDLEMEIER *(quietly to Donna)*

Good.

      (quietly to Pollock, as he gives him the cup)

Here's the elixir.

(out loud, for public consumption)

So, a little drink to celebrate your arrival?

POLLOCK
Excellent.

(lifting his glass)

To the future!

(to Needlemeier)

All of it!

(to Chorus)

Let's all drink!

Drink to the future
All of it mine
To my vast wealth
Now I add time
Drink to tomorrow
All that it brings
Tomorrow will make me
Richer than kings
Drink to the next day
And all that's ahead
If I tire of a first wife
I'll wait till she's dead
If I tire of my new friends

I'll wait till they're cold
I'll still be young
When a thousand years old

(door opens)

Shut the door!
Don't let me see
Not there!
Nowhere's worse
Than there!

SUSANNAH

He's shaking. Breaking News: Luke Pollock is having a
breakdown!

POLLOCK

Come, let's drink!
To Needlemeier!
One sup of your brew
Stamps death with its seal
I may act immortal
Now I'll do it for real
Sing praise!

NEEDLEMEIER *(to Donna)*

Look at him drink
Like it's a bottomless barrel
Like he's got forever
To piss it all away

DONNA *(to Needlemeier)*
>Look at him guzzle
>Like there's no tomorrow
>Tomorrow will feel real
>When we take his bollock away

POLLOCK *(getting more drunk and groggy)*
>Sing praise!

VILLAGERS
>Let's sing of our wonder
>At Needlemeier's skill
>And drink to his good health
>That serves us all so well
>Sing praise!

POLLOCK
>Let's drink!

NEEDLEMEIER
>Tomorrow he'll have a hangover

>*(gesturing to his groin)*

>And there'll be less hanging over than he expected

DONNA
>Tonight you'll be united

>*(gesturing to herself)*

>With every bit of me you've wanted

VILLAGERS *(getting drunk, no longer making sense, and singing in slurs)*

> Needlemeier!
> Noodle Needlemeier!
> He once cut the skin off a . . . something
> And did a thing that was good
> We can't remember the outcome
> But he was very impressive!

(Some of them collapse in a drunken heap)

POLLOCK

> Drink! Drink!

DONNA

> . . . every bit of me you've wanted

Having drunk anaesthetic, thinking he's drinking the elixir, Pollock falls unconscious and is taken off. Donna is also carted off, having drunk anaesthetic.

No. 16
Creation of Elixir

Darkness all around. A spot of light shows us the developments of Luke Pollock's operation, where his testicle is removed, and Donna's procedure, where her gashed face is replaced with that of Lania's. Needlemeier takes Pollock's testicle and adds it to the vat.

No. 17
Solo

Flitting across another part of the stage, still in a surgical gown, Robert searches for more mirrors in which to spot his reflection.

ROBERT

It's a success
I am so blessed
My great loins are aglow
With ardour below
Such perfect features
A vision of grace
I greet my lover
Adorning my face
Now I must find him
He whose looks match
Whoever has my face
Will make the perfect catch

He exits.

No. 18b
Dance of the Seven Bandages
Solo & Chorus

Lania, her face covered in bandages, but wearing a beautiful ball gown, steps forward. Assistants slowly remove her bandages. Lania slowly, and with difficulty, starts to sing, her words in a jumble.

LANIA

> Putting right right right
> My cheeks
> We'll put you down for next week
> Plump, plump
> Plump up your backside
> What cream are you using?
> No they can't be oozing
> I wish I was close to you
> My lips
> Must come off
> *Thirteen tons of human fat boiled down to the size of a*
> *pint of milk*
> Donna speaking

> > *The bandages are all off. They reveal Lania to have*
> > *Donna's old face, complete with hideous gash.*
> > *Lania is unaware of this, and walks proudly around*
> > *the room. She's looking for a mirror.*

No. 19a
Chorus & Duet

VILLAGERS

> Look!
> Hush!
> Quiet!
> Shush!

> > *Donna enters, looking like Lania.*

DONNA

    Oh Needlemeier

    Needlemeier

    My desire

    I have seen me

    All praise to you

    All praise my love

CLINIC STAFF

    What?

    But, but? —

    How come? —

LANIA *(shocked)*

    No—

DONNA

    What's the matter?

    Why do you stir?

    Have you not seen

    True beauty before?

VILLAGERS

    Another Lania?

CLINIC STAFF

    It can't be Lania

VILLAGERS

    It sounds like Donna!

CLINIC STAFF

It can't be Donna

LANIA

No, no—

DONNA

Yes
I am still Donna
Without Donna's face
Love in its fullness
Has taken Donna's place

VILLAGERS

Keep still!
No noise!

CLINIC STAFF

Listen!
Shut up!

DONNA

Lania was his first love
Donna's love more true
And now inside and out
I am Needlemeier's love
Through and through

CLINIC STAFF

Who?
Why?

What?
When?

LANIA
It can't be real

VILLAGERS
How come?

SUSANNAH *(sticking out a microphone)*
How does it feel?

No. 19b
Ensemble

Pollock enters, clearly limping.

POLLOCK
Sore
I am so sore

CLINIC STAFF / VILLAGERS
What's wrong?

POLLOCK
One of my testicles
Is no more!

(to Needlemeier)

You, you will pay

DONNA *(looking like Lania)*
> Who?

POLLOCK
> Needlemeier!
> You, you!

NEEDLEMEIER
> Me?

POLLOCK
> Needlemeier!
> I will hurt you
> I will kill you!

DONNA
> No

LANIA *(looking like Donna)*
> Yes

POLLOCK
> I will gut you
> My chef will grill you

NEEDLEMEIER
> But—

LANIA
> Yes!

DONNA
>No!

POLLOCK *(to Needlemeier and to Lania looking like Donna)*
>You—
>You two!

LANIA
>No!

DONNA
>Yes!

LANIA *(to Donna)*
>You witch!

POLLOCK *(to Lania looking like Donna)*
>You bitch!

LANIA
>Don't call me that

DONNA
>Knock her flat

POLLOCK
>You booked me here

LANIA
>I did not

NEEDLEMEIER
>It's her fault I fear

DONNA *(pointing to Lania)*
>This is Donna

LANIA
>No, it's not!

NEEDLEMEIER
>She must have made a mistake when booking you

POLLOCK
>My chef will take your head and hands and heart
>And turn them into a satisfying Irish stew

NEEDLEMEIER
>Are you talking about her or me?

POLLOCK
I'm talking about all of you!

Needlemeier and Donna drink the elixir.

NEEDLEMEIER *(to Donna)*
Quick, quick
Let's go

LANIA *(to Needlemeier)*
>Stay, stay
>You can't go

DONNA *(to Needlemeier)*
> Drink, drink
> Before we go

CLINIC STAFF / VILLAGERS
> What's wrong?

POLLOCK *(to all of them)*
> I am angry
> I am scorned
> I am furious
> I am wronged
> I am savage
> I'm enraged
> I am an actor
> In the most dreadful tragedy
> > ever staged
> I am Luke Pollock!

SUSANNAH
> *Who's lost a bollock*
>
> > *(short silence as they all look at her)*
>
> *Go on.*
>
> > *(she takes notes)*

LANIA
> Don't go
> Don't leave
> Stay here

My dear
Let's kiss
Let's laugh
Don't go
Don't leave

DONNA
Let's go
Let's leave
Disappear
My dear
We'll kiss
We'll laugh
Let's go
Let's leave

POLLOCK *(pointing to each of them)*
You sod
You mutt
You ass
You slut
You pig
You dick
You cur
You prick

NEEDLEMEIER *(to Donna)*
My joy
My life
My all
My wife
My strength

My rock
My youth

POLLOCK
My cock

SUSANNAH *(writing it all down, or speaking into her Dictaphone)*
Great twist
Fab news
Good pics
Ace views
Big story
So hot
This scoop
Has got the lot

LANIA
Remove that mask
There can't be two of me

DONNA
There's one, not two
And it isn't you

LANIA
How can I not be me?

DONNA
There's one of you, and it's me

LANIA
> You?
> Not me?

DONNA
> Me!
> Not you!

LANIA
> How can that be?

DONNA
> There's one
> Not two

LANIA *(suddenly seeing her reflection in a silver tray)*
> How can that be?

CLINIC STAFF
> Something here is wrong
> Nothing is quite right

NEEDLEMEIER *(whipping up Chorus)*
> Drink, drink, drink!

VILLAGERS
> Goodbye to lamentation
> Let's greet with celebration

LANIA *(looking at her reflection)*
> I suddenly see

NEEDLEMEIER
> Drink, drink, drink, drink!

CLINIC STAFF
> Drink, drink, drink!

LANIA
> I don't see me
> Ah!

DONNA
> Aha!

VILLAGERS
> Goodbye to—
> Let's greet with—

LANIA
> Oh! Ah!

LANIA, DONNA & NEEDLEMEIER
> Oh! Ah! Oh!

CLINIC STAFF & VILLAGERS
> Ah! Oh! Ah!

LANIA
> Ah! Oh!
> Oh! Ah!
> a!
> o!
> Do—!

SUSANNAH

Mrs Needlemeier, is there anything you'd like to say at
this tragic moment?

LANIA

—nna!?
O!
A!
Aaaaaaaaaaagh!

Avalanche starts.

DONNA & NEEDLEMEIER

The mountains quake
Head for the lake
Let's drink to—

NEEDLEMEIER

Our new life forever

DONNA

Your new wife forever

CLINIC STAFF & VILLAGERS

Aaaaaaah!

LANIA

Aaaaaaah!!

An avalanche of snow engulfs the clinic; Donna
and Needlemeier ski off.

CLINIC STAFF & VILLAGERS
> Quick, quick
> Let's drink
> Quick, quick
> Try not to think
> We must confess
> This is a mess
> Who's real, who's false
> We can only guess
> So quick, quick
> Let's drink
> Quick, quick
> Try not to think
> It's so confusing
> The plot we're losing
> We find this
> No longer amusing

No. 19c
Solo

The stage now empty, covered in snow.

ELSA
> All gone
> Father, mother, father's lover, all gone
> Their hope of finding true love all gone
> Distraught, distracted, distracted and distraught,
>   their minds have all gone
> But though I am left here, here I'll not remain
> I can find true love, I shall be the one who stays sane

Now I have Robert's new face, for me a new hope is
    sprung
He will see and love me, and to me all love and
    happiness will come

ACT THREE

*Several years later. A gated clinic on America's
West Coast. A sun-lit spa. Photos and posters of
Donna (now with Lania's face) and Robert are
everywhere, advertising good looks and cosmetics.*

    *Needlemeier's vat, now looking well-used, is in a
prominent position. There is an outside courtyard,
but it is cut off from the rest of the world by a
high wall. A large doorway is the only exit. Some
people, on loungers, are asleep.*

No. 20
Introduction & Duet

    *Night. Susannah, dressed in clinic uniform,
creeps forward into the courtyard; she has her
microphone.*

SUSANNAH DANGERFIELD
    Ages have passed and this is Susannah Dangerfield, still

*on air reporting for Global.Glamour BizzBuzz. You join
me now in sleepy California where our story resumes.*

*Luke Pollock's lying low after the cloud-capped
mountain tumbled snow. The girl who lost her boyfriend
has nowhere to go. Lania's turned from Needlemeier's
wife to bitterest foe. While Herr Doktor's potion has seen
his fortune grow.*

*Needlemeier's nervous. There are two flies in his
ointment. The elixir's running very, very low. And it
passes on Pollock's fear of the open. People come in, but
don't want to go.*

*They say they're happy. Is that why their smiles are
stuck for hours? And if it's so sunny, why's everyone
frozen?*

*It sure looks like Needlemeier's in a stew. He needs
fresh flesh, or he's dead meat.*

> *Two women on loungers stir. Elsa, looking like
> Robert, and Lania, looking like Donna, wake up*

ELSA

Donna? Donna?

LANIA

    No, I am Lania
    Robert? Robert?
    Where's my daughter?

ELSA

    Here with you
    I am Elsa

SUSANNAH
>   *Donna and Robert?*

ELSA / LANIA
>   No, Elsa and Lania

SUSANNAH
>   *Really?*

ELSA / LANIA
>   Yes

SUSANNAH
>   *Well it's nice to put a name to a face.*

ELSA / LANIA
>   Who are you?

SUSANNAH
>   *No one*
>   *Really*
>   *No one*
>   *An onlooker*
>   *Just looking*
>   *On*

ELSA
>   Mother?

LANIA
>   Daughter?

ELSA / LANIA

> Where's my / your father?

ELSA

> He lives here

LANIA

> I know he's near

ELSA

> I need him

LANIA

> I hate him

ELSA

> He can be of help

LANIA

> He can go to hell
> I am your mother
> Abandoned and ashamed
> Pursuing your father
> Furious and maimed
> Looking like a woman I have no love for
> Looking for the man I no longer love

> *(she produces a knife)*

> But I have been learning
> The knowledge of the knife
> I found a scalpel in the ruins

And lifted it to my breast
To take my own life
But then I saw his books
Learnt his skills and his spells,
That smooth wrinkles into youth
Seal time in good looks.
I have the power of a surgeon
To slice through the knot of ages

ELSA

I am your Elsa
Turned to Robert
And I will help you
If you lead me to Robert
For now my heart fills
With aching for Robert
When I find him
I will love him
Or I will end him
Whichever happens
Robert will lie down with Robert
In unending union

ELSA / LANIA

All past misdeeds
We will amend
Into these people
Must we now blend
And bring our sorrow
To a happy end

No. 21
Chorus

> *Night.*
>> *The gate opens, Chorus comes outside, looking old and ugly.*

CHORUS

Butchers and bakers and Muslims and Quakers
Bankers and Baptists and midwives and Shakers
All of us withering, drooping, diseased
All of us paying to be eternally pleased
We are the old and ugly, come here for a cure
To live here with fresh faces, safe and secure
In this city of hope, here to remain
Forever young, forever the same
Methodists and miners, actors and Sikhs
Teachers and tailors, sellers of antiques
Catholics and chemists, jockeys and Jews
Hindus and housewives, designers of shoes

> *Chorus drinks elixir; all women turn into young and beautiful Donnas with Lania's face; all men turn into Robert.*
>> *Elsa and Lania try blending in with the crowd. The real Donna also emerges, and is suspicious of these two figures; she watches them.*

Drink, drink
Drink, drink
Sink
Into youth

Sink
Into beauty
We are
The beauti-
Beauti-
Beautiful
Need
We need
Need-
Needlemeier
He is
The bounti-
Bounti-
Bountiful
Treat
We treat
We treat ourselves
To this
To this look
This look
Forever
Retreat
From outside
Retreat
Forever

*Chorus members start to panic as they notice the
gate to the outside world is still open.*

Shut the gate!
Don't let us out!
Out we hate!

We like in!
Drink, drink
Let's not think
Sing praise!

Chorus goes back inside; gate closes.

Day.

No. 22
Scene

Needlemeier approaches the vat, looking troubled.

NEEDLEMEIER
All good things come to an end
All good fruit turns bad
Oblivion scatters
Time shatters
The hope of men
Without Needlemeier
The beauty of women
Turns fallow
Without Needlemeier
Needlemeier
Needlemeier
To eternity
I aspire

Chorus moans.

This vat needs replenishing
I hear your youth diminishing
I need a female beauty
To volunteer her fat
To live immortal
As one who died
By jumping in the vat

CHORUS *(entering, looking like Donnas and Roberts)*
    Take a Donna from us
    Donna is true beauty
    Choose from two Donnas
    Which will do her duty

> *Needlemeier selects two candidates from among*
> *the Chorus of Donnas: the real Donna (with Lania's*
> *face) and a Donnalike.*

NEEDLEMEIER
    Climb upward
    Rival to rival
    Each of you sing
    For your survival

> *The two Donnas are placed on a high platform*
> *overlooking the vat.*

DONNA
    Of all the Donnas
    I am the best
    I'm the real Donna
    Choose from the rest

DONNALIKE

> I'd love to jump in
> But I think you should know
> Though I'm attractive
> I'm mentally slow

CHORUS

> Though she's attractive
> She's mentally slow

DONNA

> I'm a superb swimmer
> And I'm great in bed
> But I have a weak left ankle
> So chuck her in instead

DONNALIKE

> Don't throw me in
> Though I've considerable merit
> I've got two round shoulders
> Which you won't want to inherit

CHORUS

> She's got two round shoulders
> Which we won't want to inherit

DONNALIKE *(pointing to real Donna)*

> Let this other Donna
> Be the goner

DONNA

> No! I'm your lover –
> Choose another!

NEEDLEMEIER

> Two fine specimens
> But which one? There's the rub

(to real Donna)

> Lady, take care of your ankle

(to Donnalike)

> You, jump in the tub

Needlemeier pushes the Donnalike in.

CHORUS

> This one becomes none
> So we become one

NEEDLEMEIER *(to real Donna)*

> You, you're too good to let go
> Keep her here for later

The real Donna is led away.
Chorus drinks elixir and exits, with drooping
rounded shoulders.

No. 23
Solo

Robert enters, looking for more mirrors to examine
his image. He's had even more surgery to perfect
his features and, as a result, looks grotesque.

ROBERT

Look
Look at me, Elsa
You won't believe this is me
I have grown handsome
If you could touch me, Elsa
You would probably marvel
At skin smooth as marble
On a face to make Michelangelo cry
I am your Robert
The Robert to end all Roberts
For whom a million would willingly die

Susannah spots him and watches him from afar.

Hear
Can you hear me, Elsa?
My body is strong and lean
I am too perfect for mere mortals
A Matterhorn among midgets
An Amazon next to a stream
My beauty lights up the heavens
Brighter than the sun and the moon
I am the Robert, your Robert

From whom all Roberts bloom
I am Atlas in search of a queen

> *As Robert exits, Susannah's attention is drawn towards*
> *Luke Pollock, who emerges looking distraught and*
> *haggard, a man in personal and unending turmoil.*

No. 24
Duet

POLLOCK *(dishevelled)*

    I am a who?
    In search of a what?
    I used to be whole
    Now I am not

SUSANNAH

    A who?
    How a who?
    Not?
    All not what?

POLLOCK

    I am a poor bereft king
    Wearing a shattered crown
    I had a sceptre and two orbs
    Now one orb's gone to ground
    Come back dear ball
    You are my golden globe
    With you I have my all
    Without you I lose all hope

SUSANNAH

> *This is live footage of a broken, messed-up man.*
> *Is he a Wall Street fraudster? A brain-dead boxer?*
> *Or perhaps a runaway bishop? I smell news!*

POLLOCK

> I am a star in the descendant
> Photographers used to shout my name
> I remember the drugs and the parties
> The paternity suits and the fame
> Now I am torn from my manhood
> And I'm dazed by my loss
> Yet I know no one's interested
> And couldn't give a toss

SUSANNAH

> *Who is this moaning madman?*

POLLOCK

> I am in torment
> In a raging, blazing torment of utterly demented
>   hell

SUSANNAH *(interviewing him)*
> *So, how do you feel?*

POLLOCK

> I am inconsolable

SUSANNAH

> *Can you sum up, in just three words?*

POLLOCK

> I will die broken and incomplete, withered.
> > Intestate!

SUSANNAH

> *That's eight words. And now, make an appeal!*

POLLOCK

> I was an actor
> Now I'm just mad
> I've lost a bollock

SUSANNAH

> *That's too bad.*

POLLOCK

> *I'll marry who finds it. I'll offer my kingdom for a*
> > *gonad.*

SUSANNAH

> *He is mad. Wait, an actor? It's Pollock. We're going live,*
> *viewers, with continuous coverage of an actor looking*
> *for a part. What a scoop! Stay tuned for non-stop semi-*
> *castrated celebrity mayhem.*

No. 25
Scene

CHORUS *(entering, looking like Donnas and Roberts)*

> A world in motion
> Takes Needlemeier's potion

And stops turning
Frozen and free

NEEDLEMEIER

Hush my clientele
For all to be well
I need another sacrifice
I need a shot of muscle
I need a Robert
A supple Robert
To keep my vat moist

All the men, looking like Robert, are bundled together.

CHORUS

Take a Robert from us
From the Roberts here arrayed
Choose a Robert
Any Robert
From the million you have made

NEEDLEMEIER

Climb upward
All you rivals
Each of you sing
For your survival

Needlemeier selects two Robertalikes and the real Robert as candidates. They are led to the platform overlooking the vat. Needlemeier is on the platform with them.

ROBERTALIKE ONE

I am quite boring

ROBERTALIKE TWO

I am inbred

ROBERTALIKE ONE

I have bad breath

CHORUS

He is quite boring
He is inbred
He has bad breath

ROBERTALIKE ONE / TWO

I am inbred / I have bad breath
So chuck him in instead

ROBERT

I'm a great dancer

ELSA

I hear a voice!

ROBERT

And I've got perfect knees

ELSA

I know that voice!

ROBERT

> But there's one thing you should know
> I am far too big below

ELSA

> Too big below?
> That's a complaint I know
> That is my Robert
> My beloved Robert

> *(calling out)*

> Save my Robert!
> Save him from the vat!

> > *Lania, sensing a suitable distraction, starts climbing*
> > *the platform with her knife, intending to kill*
> > *Needlemeier from behind.*

NEEDLEMEIER

> No, ignore him
> Feed him
> Feed him to the vat
> Push him in
> I need his skin
> And all his fat

CHORUS

> He is the true Robert
> The beautiful and true
> Grab another Robert
> Any one will do

(spotting Lania close to Needlemeier with a knife)

Needlemeier –
Beware! Beware!

DONNA

Herr Doktor –
Beware!

NEEDLEMEIER

Grab her
Grab the knife
Who is she?

She is disarmed.

LANIA

A wronged wife
Come back to cut you
To carve and kill you
To slice you out of my life

NEEDLEMEIER

No, you're never Lania
That's not the face I gave her
There's anger in those eyes
Bitter poison in those cheeks
I gave her beauty and grace
Not the hate that fills this face

LANIA

Those looks you gave me
I lost them long ago
When you left me
With the face of my foe

DONNA

Throw her in

Gate opens. Night. Chorus starts turning old and ugly.

    The Roberts are led away, and replaced on the platform by Donna and Lania, with Needlemeier between them.

CHORUS

Choose for us, Needlemeier
Choose for your choir
Which one we lose
And which we gain
Who's to depart
And who remain
Who is the runt
And who is royal
Who is to keep
And who to boil

NEEDLEMEIER

Climb upward
Rival to rival
Each of you sing
For your survival

DONNA

> Why should I sing?
> Why should I yield?
> I am your lover
> And love with a passion
> That cannot be killed

LANIA

> I am all anger
> I am all rage
> I am your wronged wife
> Boiling with bitterness
> Your vat can't assuage

CHORUS

> No bitterness
> We don't want that
> Throw in the one who loves you
> Throw her in the vat

LANIA

> Listen
> Listen to your choir

DONNA

> Hush her
> Hush that liar

> *They struggle.*

CHORUS

Choose now Needlemeier
Why wait?
It's clear we'll pay for love
But not for hate

NEEDLEMEIER

The one who says she loves me
Is the best Donna I've ever done
This perfect obsessive
Into the vat
Shall rightfully be bung

Needlemeier pushes Donna into the vat.

DONNA

No, no!
Don't you know
I am Donna, the real Donna
Donna at your service
Donna speaking
How can I help you?

NEEDLEMEIER

It's her, it's she
What am I to do?

DONNA

Let me put you through

LANIA

Why don't you jump in too!

Needlemeier, with Lania's help, jumps in after
Donna.

ELSA
It adds to the stew

POLLOCK
What's a man to do?

NEEDLEMEIER *(from inside the vat)*
No, no!
Turmoil untold!

DONNA
Can I put you on hold?

No. 26
Finale

Chorus starts drinking from the vat.

CHORUS
Drink, drink
Let's drink
Liquid Needlemeier

NEEDLEMEIER
Think! Think!
Think what will happen
Now I've fallen in the vat
You'll inherit my flaws

And my failings
My bad back
My flat feet
My foul temper
My crooked teeth
My jealous mind
My swollen head
My constant deceit
My—

DONNA

His flatulence in bed

NEEDLEMEIER

You don't want that
And what about her?
Her pettiness and vanity
Her hatred of children
Her—

DONNA

His unbounded greed
His inhumanity
His—

CHORUS *(drinking elixir)*

Feed, feed
Let's feed
Feed on Needlemeier

The elixir slowly runs out.

ELSA / LANIA

> The vat is almost empty
> My father's / My husband's schemes are foiled

NEEDLEMEIER *(out of sight)*

> I'm all melted
> My genius is boiled

ELSA / LANIA

> Look
> There's no more elixir
> Eternity no longer flows

> > *Susannah peers into the vat and finds a small,*
> > *round fleshy object.*

SUSANNAH

> *Look, over here – here's breaking news. I've found, at the*
> *bottom of the vat, this tiny, tiny, round ... ugh!*

POLLOCK

> My bollock
> You've found my bollock
> You incredible woman
> My future wife
> You've found me and completed me
> The world will stop for our wedding
> We'll tour its châteaux and chat shows
> As the planet's greatest lovers
> We'll dine with royalty and celebrity chefs
> Smile hand in hand at a million fans
> For eternity from every front cover

Oh perfect orb
One true sphere
Golden globe
That I hold dear
Now replaced
Within its sack
All wrong is righted
My power is back
I am whole, I am all
You shall go to the ball

SUSANNAH

It's very small.

POLLOCK

With this re-inserted
I shall become whole
Come lovely wife
Let's go to get married
And turn even from odd
Let's join in perfect union

SUSANNAH

Like two peas in a pod.

LANIA *(to Elsa)*

Speaking of which …

*She drops the front of the vat to reveal Donna and
Needlemeier as two large balls of flesh.*

ELSA

Good God!

NEEDLEMEIER

It is finished

DONNA

You look terrible

NEEDLEMEIER

You don't look great

DONNA

Really?
Would make-up hide it?

NEEDLEMEIER

I don't think so

DONNA

Don't wear striped clothes
They emphasise the roundness of the belly

NEEDLEMEIER

I'm not sure I'd find anything to fit

BOTH

Well, well, well
What a story to tell
Of two who rose and fell
Pell-mell
Into a kind of hell

And of hell we'll tell
'Til the tolling of the bell
Tolls our death knell
In front of our clientele

CHORUS

Donna and Needlemeier
Run through our veins
We have her beauty
And possess his brains

DONNA

Oh look at us
We're a couple of swells

NEEDLEMEIER

I don't feel well

They are both rolled offstage.
Chorus starts dropping onto the floor,
dispersing, turning old and ugly. As they do so, they
slowly move out of the city walls.

CHORUS

Fall, fall
We are falling
Falling apart
Become many peoples
Jews and Gentiles
Romans and Greeks
Tutsis and Shi'ites
Serbs and Sheikhs

No. 27
Chorus

CHORUS

    Tinker, tailor, joker, jailer
    All of us older, uglier and paler
    Tourists and day-trippers
    Communists and strippers
    Take to their walking sticks
    Bad teeth and inhalers
    Out into the world we stumble again
    To find new love wherever we can

        (starting to move off the stage and heading
        towards the audience)

    Buddhists and bricklayers
    Gypsies and jazz-players
    Chinese and Greeks
    Goalies and geeks
    Transsexual fantasists
    Teachers and profs
    Farmers and pharmacists
    Townies and toffs

        Now in among the audience, some Chorus
        members pick out members of the audience and
        sing solo lines to them.

FEMALE CHORUS MEMBER

> This one looks weird
> His hair's quite a mess

MALE CHORUS MEMBER

> She's got wonky eyes
> But I'd settle for less

FEMALE

> Here's my Prince Charming
> Though he's a bit of a klutz

MALE

> I've found my true love
> Though she's allergic to nuts

FEMALE

> He's no George Clooney

MALE

> More like Mickey Rooney

CHORUS *(spreading further out)*

> Let's scatter our seed
> All over the land
> With misfits and mavericks
> The odd and the bland
> Sopranos and basses
> Can have funny faces
> Ministers and mountaineers
> Can have sticky-out ears
> An attorney general

Has looks ephemeral
While the UN High Commissioner for Famine
    Relief
Can have buck teeth

Only Lania, Elsa and Robert are left onstage.

LANIA

    And I can become queen again
    Though wronged as a wife
    My face stays broken
    I stay forsaken
    But what is now mended
    Is the rest of my life

No. 28
Trio

ROBERT

    Elsa looks ungainly

ELSA

    Robert looks unsightly

BOTH

    We both look ugly
    But that can't stop us

ELSA

    Though your lips are scarred

ROBERT

Though your face is gashed

ELSA

Though your skin is tight

ROBERT

Though your cheeks are slashed

BOTH

I will still love you
Once we've had our surgery reversed

ELSA *(picking up Lania's knife)*

My mother can undo us
She can restore us to our glory

BOTH

Rewind our tale to its beginning
And live a happier story

LANIA

No!
I will not tamper with your looks!

ELSA

But I have false cheeks

ROBERT

My face is a mess

ELSA

Look at me

ROBERT

She's pretty ugly

LANIA

But you will love her none the less
Your desire to have her as your lover
Outweighs your desire to perfect her
The love you need to show her
Is a love that grows each day
Not a love withering in falsehood
But thriving and contending
With whatever fate throws her way

ROBERT

True

ELSA

Dull, but true

ROBERT

I love you

ELSA

I look like you

BOTH

As long as I have you
Your looks will do
Let's not think of forever

But just this day we're together
Let's not tamper with time passing
But meet him for the moment
Let's just linger
Never hunger
For a future
When we're never dead
Let's just stay here
Growing older
Let's be happy
Let's go to get wed
Let's go to our bed

> *They leave, as night falls. Lania is left alone onstage.*

Credits

Use Your Ears: BBC Radio 3, 18 August 2004

Shuffling towards a New Age: *Gramophone*, August 2006

Falling on Deaf Ears: *Gramophone*, May 2007

Coffee and Surprises: *Gramophone*, August 2007

Making the Grade: *The Times*, June 2016

Speechless?: *Gramophone*, September 2008

Classicool: *Gramophone*, March 2007

Surprisingly Ugly: *Gramophone*, Awards 2008

Hear Me Out: extracts from a speech to the Royal
   Philharmonic Society, *Observer*, 14 May 20016

The Big Tune: *Gramophone*, April 2007

Words into Music: *Gramophone*, December 2006

The Museum of Lost Keyboards: BBC Radio 3, 13
   December 2003

Who the Hell Was Malcolm Arnold?: *Gramophone*,
   November 2006

Modernism and Knees-Ups: *Gramophone*, February 2007

By Special Arrangement: *Gramophone*, June 2007

A Sense of an Ending: *Gramophone*, July 2007

Going Solo: *Gramophone*, May 2008

Beyond a Joke: *Gramophone*, April 2009

Living with Mahler: BBC Radio 3, 14 August 2005

Finding Schumann: *Gramophone*, December 2007

Bach in Space: *Gramophone*, January 2008

Unheard Of: *Gramophone*, March 2008

How Good is Mozart?: *Gramophone*, April 2008

Rameau's on his Own: *Gramophone*, January 2007

Four Movements: *Gramophone*, October 2006

The Shadow of Death: *Gramophone*, Awards 2006

Silence and Sibelius: *Gramophone*, October 2007

A Life at the Opera: from *Facts and Fancies* (London: Penguin, 1997)

War Weary: *Gramophone*, July 2008

The Special One: *Gramophone*, June 2008

Now's the Right Time for John Adams: *Gramophone*, August 2008

Keeping it Simple: *Gramophone*, November 2008

Taverner v Tavener: *Gramophone*, January 2009

... and Repeat: *Gramophone*, March 2009

Mobile Phones Off: BBC Radio 3, 2004

Twice is Nice: *Gramophone*, November 2007

In Sequence: *Gramophone*, Awards 2007

Skin Deep: introduction *Gramophone*, February 2009